PREDATOR
ANIMALS WITH THE SKILL TO KILL

PREDATOR

ANIMALS WITH THE SKILL TO KILL

by
Steve Setford

Consultant
David Burnie

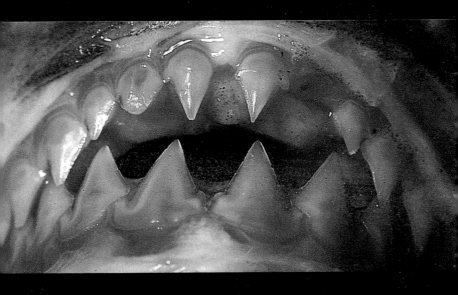

A DK Publishing Book

Dorling   Kindersley

LONDON, NEW YORK, MUNICH,
MELBOURNE, and DELHI

Project Editor Steve Setford
Project Art Editor Peter Radcliffe
Senior Editor Fran Jones
Senior Art Editor Stefan Podhorodecki
Category Publisher Linda Martin
Managing Art Editor Jane Thomas
Picture Researcher Sean Hunter
US Editors Christine Heilman, Margaret Parrish
DK Picture Library Gemma Woodward, Hayley Smith
Production Jenny Jacoby
DTP Designer Siu Yin Ho

First American Edition, 2003
03 04 05 06 07 10 9 8 7 6 5 4 3 2 1

Published in the United States by
DK Publishing, Inc.
375 Hudson Street
New York, New York 10014

A Cataloging-in-Publication record for this book is available
from the Library of Congress

ISBN 0-7894-9705-0 (hc)
ISBN 0-7894-9224-5 (pb)

Reproduced by Colourscan, Singapore
Printed and bound in Italy by L.E.G.O.

See our complete product line at
www.dk.com

CONTENTS

INTRODUCTION

A snake's scaly coils squeeze the life out of a pig, a tiger's teeth rip at a deer's flesh, a scorpion's stinger injects lethal poison into a lizard—the natural world is often extremely violent. That's because many animals are predators, which have to kill for food. Predators and prey, the animals they hunt, are locked in a daily struggle for survival that's both gruesome and utterly fascinating.

Predators are natural-born killers—they hunt not by choice but by instinct. This is a type of built-in behavior that an animal inherits from its parents, and it ensures that from the moment most predators are born, they know everything they need to about the killing game. Mammal predators and some birds are exceptions to this. They, too, are born with the urge to kill, but their parents have to teach them how to hunt. In fact, the cubs of polar bears, tigers, and lions

THE ORNATE HORNED FROG DOESN'T BOTHER TO KILL ITS VICTIMS, BUT SWALLOWS THEM WHOLE.

spend at least 2 years "training" before they are skilled enough to survive on their own.

This book will take you on an incredible journey deep into predator territory. But hold on tight—it's a bloody, messy, bone-crunching ride. Read about the amazing powers of detection that enable predators to track down their prey. Learn about the different tactics, traps, and tricks that nature's exterminators use to catch themselves a meal. Shudder at the range of spine-chilling weapons that predators use to dispatch their victims. And discover that the hunters don't have it all their own way, because nature equips prey animals with a host of incredible survival skills to help them avoid being eaten.

For those of you who want to explore the subject in more detail, there are "Log On" boxes that appear throughout this book. These will direct you to some great websites where you can find even more information about predators. So turn the pages—and get your teeth into the book!

Steve Setford

THE KILLING GAME

A group of elephant seals basks on a sun-kissed beach while their pups play at the water's edge. Suddenly, a huge orca, or killer whale, erupts from the surf and snatches one of the surprised pups in its jaws. It wriggles back down the shingle into the sea with its squealing prey. The pup is tossed in the air, shaken violently, and then swallowed whole. Welcome to the world of predators!

This grisly, heart-rending scene is just one of many millions that occur every day as vast numbers of animals meet their doom at the hands—or, more accurately, the claws, teeth, fangs, and stingers—of predators. It may seem cruel and nasty to us but, like it or not, it's just the way things are in nature.

Living lunches

To put it in a nutshell, the story of predators is about the quest for food. All animals need

food, because it supplies them with nutrients for building up their bodies, and also with energy to make their bodies work. The creatures we call predators are carnivores (meat-eaters), and they obtain their nutrients and energy from the flesh of other animals, which they catch and then eat. So the next time you come across a picture of a predator devouring its prey and think, "Ugh! How horrible," try to remember that it's just an animal having lunch.

ONE DEAD ORCA HAD 14 PORPOISES AND BITS OF 14 SEALS IN ITS BELLY

AN ORCA SURGES UP THE BEACH AND GRABS AN ELEPHANT SEAL ON THE COAST OF PATAGONIA IN SOUTHERN ARGENTINA.

Food chains and food webs

In the natural world, every plant and animal is potential food. Animals called herbivores eat plants, while carnivores need to eat meat to survive. Even when living things die, their remains can provide nourishment for organisms called detrivores, which include earthworms, bacteria, and fungi. In this way, nutrients and energy pass on from one organism to the next, in a series of links called a food chain. Grass, for example, provides food for the reindeer, which in turn is eaten by the gray wolf. The gray wolf is at the "top" of this food chain, because it has no natural predators. Most animals eat a range of foods (in the case of predators, that means a range of prey), so they fit into more than one food chain. The result is a network of interlinked food chains called a food web.

GRAY WOLVES CAN'T SURVIVE ON PLANT FOOD, AND DIE IF THEY DON'T GET MEAT TO EAT.

A GRIZZLY PLUCKS A LEAPING SALMON FROM THE AIR WITH ITS JAWS. GRIZZLIES ARE OMNIVORES, MEANING THAT THEY EAT BOTH PLANTS AND ANIMALS.

LOG ON...
http://sirtf.caltech.edu/
Education//Zoo/coldwarm.html

Part-time killers

Some predators, such as gray wolves, exist entirely on meat. Others, including the grizzly bear, adapt their diet according to what's available. The grizzly preys on wild sheep, moose, deer, small mammals, frogs, and fish. It's also happy to feed on nuts, shoots, berries, buds, and fruit when they're in season, and eat roots and bulbs that it digs up with its claws.

The giant panda, the grizzly's relative, eats almost nothing but bamboo, chomping through an amazing 84 lb (38 kg) of the stuff each day. The panda will occasionally catch rodents or reptiles, but its slow, heavy body makes it an inefficient predator. Consequently, the panda rarely gets the chance to eat meat.

Feeding times

Even "full-time" meat-eaters only kill when they have to. How regularly they feed varies from species to species. But in general, warm-blooded predators eat more frequently than cold-blooded ones. For example, a warm-blooded shrew eats every 3–4 hours, while a cold-blooded, bird-eating spider of a similar size can go for weeks between meals.

The reason for this is that warm-blooded animals—birds and mammals—use most of the energy from their food to warm their bodies. This lets them stay active, whatever the temperature around them. In contrast, cold-blooded animals—which make up all the rest—stay just as cold or warm as their surroundings. Because they don't use food for warmth, they need less energy, and thus less food.

The hunting life

Both warm- and cold-blooded carnivores spend far less time feeding than plant-eaters. That's because nutrients and energy are more concentrated in meat than they are in plants. A wildebeest's flesh, for example, contains about 100 times more protein than the grass it eats.

11

Wildebeest have to graze on grass for up to 18 hours per day to get the nourishment they need, while lions, which often eat wildebeest, spend about the same amount of time resting.

But a lion's life isn't as easy as it seems. Chasing prey uses up a lot of energy, so the lion needs these long rest periods to recover from its exertions. This rest time is vital, because fewer than one in five of a lion's hunts may result in a kill.

One reason for this lack of success is that there's so much more at stake for the prey than the predator. If the predator doesn't come out on top, so what? There'll soon be another chance to make a killing. But for the prey, it's a case of escape or die. That's why the prey will risk using up all its energy to flee from an attacker, or even try fighting back. Hunters often give up if the prey fights back. An injury could prevent a predator from hunting and cause it to starve, or a wound might get infected and be fatal.

R aider from the sky

Because of the time, effort, and risks involved in catching prey, most predators will steal a meal from another animal if they get the chance. Some are more

LIONS MAY GO ON SEVERAL UNSUCCESSFUL HUNTS BEFORE BRINGING DOWN PREY.

skilled at this than others. The tropical frigate bird has found that there are rich pickings to be had by bullying other birds into surrendering their catch of food. It dive-bombs birds such as gulls, boobies, and petrels, flapping wildly, pecking at their wings, and even shaking their tail feathers. In order to escape, the victim coughs up its meal, which the frigate bird snatches in midair and gulps down. Swallowing someone else's regurgitated grub may not be to our taste, but it doesn't bother the frigate bird one bit.

S trength in numbers

Spotted hyenas use similar bullying tactics on Africa's grasslands. They are formidable hunters in their own right, but if a group of hyenas finds a cheetah or jackal with a fresh kill, they'll threaten and harass it until it abandons its quarry. A large pack can even drive a pair of lions away from their food.

Hyenas are also well-known scavengers, eating the scraps left behind by other animals, plus the parts they can't digest. They're well adapted for this— their massive jaws can crunch up and chew gristle, skin, and bone. When they finish with a wildebeest carcass, the only parts left are the horns!

Nature's garbage collectors

Vultures, too, are experts at scavenging. They occasionally take live prey, but usually prefer to dine on carrion—the meat of a dead animal. Soaring high in the sky, vultures can spot a carcass from several miles away. There are six species of vultures on Africa's grasslands, and each specializes in eating a different part of the carcass. Like hyenas, they do a valuable job by clearing away animal remains.

Predators or parasites?

Unlike predators, parasitic animals live on or in the body of another animal, and use it as a living food source. But some

VULTURES AND SPOTTED HYENAS PICK OVER A WILDEBEEST CARCASS.

THIS VAMPIRE BAT HAS PIERCED THE SKIN OF A PIG'S TEAT AND IS LAPPING UP BLOOD.

animals—particularly blood drinkers—behave like a cross between the two. They steal a meal from their "prey" and then make a quick exit to digest their ill-gotten gains undisturbed. The vampire bat, for example, takes to the sky at night and uses its razor-sharp teeth to puncture the skin of sleeping animals. It then laps up the blood that seeps from the wound. The amount of blood drunk by the bat rarely endangers the animal's life. It's not in the bat's interest to kill its victim, because it would then lose its food source.

In the natural world it seems that, alive or dead, there's always a creature ready to make a meal out of you!

WEIRD WORLD

BLOOD IS HIGH IN PROTEIN BUT LOW IN ENERGY. A VAMPIRE BAT USES UP A LOT OF ENERGY IN FLIGHT, SO IT NEEDS TO DRINK 60 PERCENT OF ITS OWN BODY WEIGHT EACH DAY IN BLOOD. IF IT DOESN'T FEED FOR TWO DAYS, IT WILL DIE.

SENSES FOR SLAYING

A predator that can't find food won't last long. Over millions of years, nature's killers have developed a sophisticated array of prey-detecting sensors to help them root out prey, wherever it may be lurking. The sight, smell, hearing, touch, and taste of many predators are far better than our own, and some hunters have extra senses that we don't possess. These super-senses ensure that there's no hiding place for the hunted.

A WOLF SPIDER HAS EIGHT EYES, BUT USES TWO LARGE, MAIN EYES TO FOCUS ON PREY.

See you for dinner

Sharp eyesight can give a hunter a crucial advantage over its prey. A peregrine falcon, for example, can spot a pigeon from 5 miles (8 km) away—long before the falcon comes within range of the pigeon's eyes. The key to the falcon's amazing vision lies in the retina. This is a special layer at the back of the eyes of birds and other vertebrates (animals with backbones).

The retina contains millions of light-sensitive cells known as photoreceptors. The more densely packed these cells are, the more detailed an image the animal sees. The retinas of birds of prey such as falcons are up to five times more densely packed with light-sensitive cells than our own. This is why they can see so much better than us.

Like most other hunters that find prey by sight, falcons have two forward-facing eyes at the front of the head. When the predator spots its prey, each eye sees the animal from a different angle. The brain merges the two views to give a 3-D image. This is called stereoscopic vision, and it allows the predator to judge distances accurately as it dives, leaps, or charges at its victims.

Murder by moonlight

Nocturnal predators have only the moon and stars to hunt by, so they have especially large eyes to let in the

THE GOLDEN EAGLE, A BIRD OF PREY, CAN SPOT ANIMALS SUCH AS FOXES FROM A DISTANCE OF 1.25 MILES (2 KM).

two different types of eyes. The most primitive type, called simple eyes, can detect the difference between light and dark, but can't form images. That job is left to the insect's two bizarre-looking compound eyes.

These are made up of a number of six-sided structures called ommatidia, each of which contains a tiny lens. The insect's brain combines the data from all the different ommatidia to produce a mosaic-like view made up of dozens or even thousands of small images.

Insects don't see in as much detail as we do, but they are far better at noticing movement. A dragonfly's motion detection is so good that it can even make

maximum amount of light. An owl's eyes are so good at capturing light that it can make out an object in just 1 percent of the light that we'd need to see the same thing.

Owls, in common with cats, hyenas, and other night hunters, have a reflective layer called a tapetum behind the retina. Light rays strike the mirrorlike tapetum and reflect back through the retina, giving the photoreceptors another chance to capture every last glimmer.

Loads of lenses

Insect eyes are nothing like those of vertebrates. For a start, insects have

SOME DRAGONFLIES HAVE UP TO
30,000 OMMATIDIA IN EACH OF
THEIR COMPOUND EYES.

WEIRD WORLD

MOST ANIMAL EYES CONTAIN A LENS THAT CHANGES SHAPE TO ADJUST THE EYE'S FOCUS. BUT THE LENSES IN INSECT EYES CAN'T CHANGE SHAPE, SO IF AN INSECT WANTS TO SEE SOMETHING MORE CLEARLY, IT MUST MOVE CLOSER.

out the individual wingbeats of its prey at a rate of up to 300 per second. (Any more than 50 beats per second is a blur to the human eye.) This enables the dragonfly to track every twist and turn of its quarry during aerial pursuits, and to determine the prey's exact direction and speed as it zooms in to strike.

Vision and brain power

Although ultra-sensitive to motion, many small predators, including dragonflies and toads, don't have the brain power to recognize non-moving objects as food. Identifying the shapes and patterns of prey requires a more sophisticated brain than they possess.

TO TRACK PREY, THE CARACAL CAN ROTATE ITS LARGE EARS INDEPENDENTLY OF EACH OTHER THROUGH 180°.

A toad won't touch a fly if it stays still, for example, because it doesn't realize that there's a tasty snack right under its nose. But as soon as the fly moves— zap!—the toad shoots out its tongue and the fly is history.

Ears are an asset

Sharp eyesight doesn't always guarantee a meal. What happens when prey is lying low, out of sight? That's when a good pair of ears comes in handy. Many hunters, including cats such as caracals and servals, and fennec

LONG-EARED BATS
USE ECHOLOCATION
TO CATCH MOTHS,
FLIES, MOSQUITOES,
AND MIDGES.

S ound scanners

Insect-eating bats, too, are ace night hunters. Flying at up to 40 mph (64 km/h), a bat can catch 900 insects per hour. This amazing tally is down to an inbuilt scanning system called echolocation. The bat sends

and bat-eared foxes, have huge earflaps to channel as much sound as possible into the ears. They can also swivel their ears around to monitor the airwaves for the telltale sound of prey.

Having two ears, one on either side of the head, enables a predator to pinpoint noises made by prey. Sound reaches one ear a split second before the other. There's also a tiny difference in volume, because sound registers louder in the closer ear. These differences tell a predator where a sound is coming from—and where prey may be hiding. Barn owls have such sensitive ears that they can locate a mouse at night using sound alone.

out brief pulses of high-pitched sound, beyond the range of human hearing. When a sound strikes a flying insect, an echo bounces back to the bat's ears. Its brain analyzes the echoes to find the flight path needed to intercept the prey. The bat scoops up the insect with its wings or tail, and stuffs it into its eager mouth.

Dolphins, orcas, and other toothed whales have their own echolocation systems to help them find prey in the ocean. A dolphin makes a series of high-pitched clicks that its

bulging forehead concentrates
into a narrow beam of sound.
The returning echoes are picked
up by its lower jaw and relayed,
via the inner ear, to the brain.
The echoes not only tell the

IN A LIFETIME, SOME BATS MAY EAT UP TO 15 MILLION INSECTS

dolphin the location, speed, and size of an animal, but they also reveal its body structure and texture, helping the dolphin to identify potential prey. Atlantic spotted dolphins can even use their echolocation to "see" fish

and other creatures hiding under sand and mud on the seafloor.

Heat scanners
Snakes of the pit viper, python, and boa families use a different type of scanning system in their quest for food. They have organs on their heads called heat pits, which can sense tiny differences in the temperature

A DOLPHIN'S ECHOLOCATION GIVES IT A DETAILED "SOUND PICTURE" OF ITS SURROUNDINGS AND HELPS IT TO IDENTIFY OBSTACLES AND PREY—SUCH AS THIS TASTY SHOAL OF FISH.

of their surroundings caused by the warmth given off by animal bodies. Lined with heat-sensitive cells called thermoreceptors, the heat pits are able to register temperature differences as small as 0.4°F (0.2°C), and locate prey up to 18 in (46 cm) away. Using its heat pits, a snake can accurately judge its prey's range and position, even at night.

Remarkable noses

Even if your enemy can't see or hear you, bounce echoes off you, or detect your body heat, it's sure to be able to smell you. Nearly every animal gives off odors, and some predators have such a great sense of smell that they can locate prey from afar.

Inside an animal's nose are special scent-detecting cells called smell receptors. The nose of a dog contains up to 50 times more smell receptors than the human nose. In fact, dogs are up to 1 million times more sensitive to some odors than we are. Wolves have the most highly developed sense of smell of all dogs. Gray wolves, for example, can detect a moose's airborne scent from more than 1.5 miles (2.5 km) away.

As impressive as this sounds, it's nothing compared to the smelling powers of the polar bear, which can sniff out a seal from a distance of up to 20 miles (32 km). However, this is on the open ice, where there are

A POLAR BEAR FEASTS ON THE BODY OF A SEAL. IT EATS ONLY THE BLUBBER AND SKIN, IGNORING THE REST OF THE CARCASS.

SCENT IS USEFUL TO PREDATORS SUCH AS THIS MONITOR LIZARD, BECAUSE THE SMELL LINGERS LIKE A SIGNPOST LONG AFTER THE PREY HAS MOVED ON.

no obstacles to prevent smells from being carried a long way by the wind. There are also few other scents in the air to distract the bear. But if the bear is upwind, it's a different story altogether. Even if the bear is just a few hundred yards away, it may miss the scent and go hungry.

For aquatic hunters such as sharks, smells travel through water. Up to one-third of a shark's brain is devoted to smell, which is why sharks are often known as "swimming noses." Experts think that some sharks may be able to smell blood at the strength of one part blood to 1 billion parts seawater. But to detect it, the shark must be down-current of the scent. If it's not, it will be unaware that there is a meal in the vicinity—just like the bear on the ice.

Extra scent sense
Snakes and some lizards, such as monitors and Gila monsters, have an extra dimension to their scent-detecting powers.

As they search for food, they not only smell through their nostrils but also flick out their forked tongues to "taste" the air. The tongue collects airborne scent particles and transfers them to a pit in the roof of the mouth called the Jacobson's organ. These scent particles provide chemical clues to the location of nearby prey.

Touching moments
Another crucial hunting sense is touch. Wading birds such as oystercatchers and curlews have long, slender, touch-sensitive bills to probe deeply into mud for worms, crabs, and mollusks. Other predators use touch-sensitive hairs to find their food.

WEIRD WORLD
HEAT PITS HELP SNAKES TO HUNT EFFICIENTLY. IN TESTS, A BLIND RATTLESNAKE HIT TARGETS 98 PERCENT OF THE TIME. ITS STRIKE RATE FELL TO 27 PERCENT WHEN ITS HEAT PITS WERE COVERED.

A walrus, for example, has up to 500 of them on its "mustache," which it uses to root around on the seabed for mussels, clams, and cockles. It can feed in complete darkness under the ice during the long Arctic winter.

Detecting vibrations

Even if a predator can't find its prey by touch, it may be able to sense vibrations that the animal creates when it moves. This is sense is sometimes described as "distant touch."

A scorpion, for example, has poor eyesight and hearing, and minimal senses of smell and taste. But the feet of moving prey, such as insects and small reptiles, can set up tiny earth tremors that the scorpion is able to pick up with sensors on its own feet. As the scorpion stalks its victim, it pauses every now and again to get a new vibrational "fix" on its target.

Ripples in water can also say "soup's on!" to hunters. An insect called the pondskater stands on the surface of pools and ponds, supported by pads of water-repellent hairs on its legs. When a fly falls into the water it sends out ripples that the pondskater detects with its legs. Quick as a flash, the pondskater scoots over to the splashdown site. But the pondskater is no lifeguard—it has murder in mind! Arriving at the scene, it administers the kiss of death by jabbing its needle-like mouthparts into the struggling fly.

Vibrations underwater can be just as much of a giveaway as surface ripples. When a sea creature swims, the movement of its body creates

IN POOR VISIBILITY, THE SWORDFISH'S LATERAL LINE ALERTS IT TO THE PRESENCE OF NEARBY PREY.

vibrations in the water around it. Fish can detect these watery wobbles with their lateral line system. This consists of a horizontal canal running along each side of the body under the skin. Each canal is lined with receptor cells that are sensitive organs on the head and lower jaw. These organs, called ampullae of Lorenzini, enable sharks to make a kill in murky water, and help skates and rays to sense the presence of buried shellfish, crabs, and worms as they cruise over the seabed.

LOG ON...
http://faculty.washington.edu/chudler/amaze.html

Combined senses

When a predator hunts, its senses usually work together. For example, a great white shark can

THE DOTS ON THE SNOUT OF THIS GREAT WHITE SHARK ARE THE PREDATOR'S ELECTROSENSE ORGANS.

to changes in water pressure caused by vibrations traveling through water. Most predatory fish use their lateral line to help them find food.

Electrosense

Sharks, skates, and rays have another amazing ability—they can detect tiny electrical pulses produced by the muscles of prey animals. It's all thanks to sensory cells known as electroreceptors in pick up sounds made by prey up to 3,300 ft (1,000 m) away. At about 1,650 ft (500 m), the nostrils lock on to the scent. Some 650 ft (200 m) from the source, the lateral line senses vibrations in the water. With 65 ft (20 m) to go, the great white's eyes locate the victim. As the shark opens its jaws, its eyes roll back in their sockets out of harm's way. Visual contact is lost, but the electrosense guides the shark to deliver a devastating bite. Dinner is served!

ARMED FOR THE KILL

I magine you're a predator. You've used your amazing sensory powers to locate your prey, and you're within striking distance, but now what? Nature's killers are equipped with a wide range of body parts for catching and dispatching victims with the minimum of fuss. From teeth that slice to claws that slash and paws that bash, the list makes terrifying reading!

Terrible teeth

Say the word predator, and most people will think of teeth—big, sharp, scary ones. And teeth don't come any scarier than those of the great white shark. Its jaws are lined with razor-sharp, serrated teeth that

TO EAT A SLIPPERY, WRIGGLING FISH, A CROCODILE HOLDS THE PREY WITH ITS PEG-LIKE TEETH AND THEN MANEUVERS IT INTO A SUITABLE POSITION TO SWALLOW.

Toothy trap

Not all hunters—not even all sharks—have such vicious dental equipment. The shape of an

SOME SHARKS GO THROUGH 30,000 TEETH BEFORE THEY DIE

resemble steak knives. As the jaws clamp together, the lower teeth pin the prey while the upper teeth carve out a chunk of flesh up to 20 lb (9 kg) in weight. A shake of the head frees the meat from the body, and the shark gulps it down.

SAID TO BE AS HARD AS GRANITE AND AS STRONG AS STEEL, A GREAT WHITE'S TEETH SEVER SKIN, MUSCLE, AND BONE WITH EASE.

animal's teeth depends on its diet and lifestyle. Skates and rays, for example, have blunt, flat teeth for crunching shellfish. The Nile crocodile, on the other hand, has conical, peg-like teeth. Small prey such as fish are impaled and swallowed whole. But because the crocodile's teeth aren't designed for cutting up flesh, larger victims present

carcasses into bite-sized chunks is easy for the crocodile, because the muscles that close its jaws are immensely powerful.

Replacement teeth

The teeth of many vertebrates, including crocodiles and sharks, are continually replaced by new ones throughout the animal's life. In crocodiles, for example, each tooth is replaced every 6–24 months. By the time it's fully grown, a Nile crocodile may already have used 45 sets of teeth—very costly for the tooth fairy!

When it comes to teeth, there's both bad and good news for mammal predators. The bad news is that most mammals only get two sets of teeth—when the second set is gone, there are no more replacements waiting in the wings. An old, toothless predator is unable to "gum" its prey to death, so it eventually

more of a problem. So the crocodile grabs a leg or other body part and spins around like a corkscrew to twist off a swallowable lump. Ripping up entire

starves. The good news, however, is that mammals have the most sophisticated gnashers in the animal world.

Different teeth, different jobs

Most mammal predators have five main types of teeth. At the front of the jaw are incisors—chisel-shaped teeth for cutting and nibbling flesh from bones. On either side of the incisors are long, pointed canine teeth for gripping and piercing. Behind these are the premolars and molars, which grind and crush food. True carnivores such as dogs and cats have carnassial teeth between the

A TIGER CARRIES A DEAD DEER THROUGH THE FOREST, GRIPPING THE CARCASS WITH ITS LONG CANINE TEETH.

molars and premolars. These overlap to slice through meat.

Drink up your dinner

Insect predators don't have teeth but they do have jawlike mouthparts. Flesh-eaters such as praying mantises, ground beetles, and ants have serrated, chopping "jaws" that work like shears to dismember prey.

Assassin bugs, robberflies, and some other insect hunters do the job differently—they drink the bodies of their prey! These tiny terrors have needlelike mouthparts that they thrust into their victims. They pump saliva and digestive fluids into the prey to liquidize its body tissue, and then suck up the yucky mush.

29

A KINGFISHER CAN SWALLOW FISH HALF AS LONG AS ITS OWN BODY

Bills for kills

Birds, too, lack teeth but they do have bills, and these are equally powerful weapons. The marabou stork usually eats carrion, but it also uses its huge, pointed beak like a sword to stab living prey such as flamingoes. Similarly, the gray heron spears small fish and frogs with quick thrusts of its long, slender bill.

Bills are also used to capture prey. The Eurasian kingfisher, for example, plunges headfirst into rivers and streams to snatch fish with its bill in spectacular splash-and-grab raids. Back on its perch in the trees, the bird stuns the fish by whacking it on a branch. The kingfisher wins by a knockout, and swallows the dazed fish with one gulp.

HAVING CAUGHT A FISH, THIS KINGFISHER WILL USE POWERFUL WINGBEATS TO STRUGGLE FREE OF THE WATER.

Eagles and other birds of prey have sharp, hooked beaks. Despite their fierce-looking appearance, the bills aren't usually used for killing. They're less like daggers and more a knife and fork—they're used for tearing flesh into bite-sized pieces that can be swallowed.

Talon-tipped toes

The real murder weapons of a bird of prey are the inward-curving, needle-sharp talons on the tips of its toes. When the bird strikes, the toes close around the prey and drive the talons deep into the victim's flesh. If the prey isn't fatally wounded, it's usually crushed to death by the sheer force of the toes' viselike grip as the bird carries it back to its nest. Struggling is useless, since it only works the talons deeper into the victim's body, where they fatally damage the spinal cord or vital organs.

Claws and paws

Eagles aren't the only animals that use their feet and claws to lethal effect. A cat's front claws are normally withdrawn into protective sheaths in the paws so that they aren't worn down as the cat walks or runs. But when it attacks, the claws extend to form hooklike tools, which dig into an animal's body so that the cat can restrain its prey. Big cats use their claws to cling to larger prey as they try to make a killing bite to the neck. In the

LOG ON...
www.bearbiology.com/specdesc.html

A BALD EAGLE DIGS THE HOOKED TIP OF ITS BILL INTO PREY AND YANKS ITS HEAD BACK TO RIP OPEN THE BODY.

process, the claws rip raking flesh wounds that weaken the animal's resistance.

Dogs also use the paws-and-claws combination to hold prey while their teeth and jaws go about the business of killing. The claws of dogs don't retract, so they tend to be fairly blunt. But the rear claw on the forelegs (the "dew claw") is high up on the foot, so it isn't used when walking. It remains sharp and can inflict a nasty injury.

A GRIZZLY USES ITS HUGE PAWS TO TACKLE LARGE PREY AND TO DEFEND ITSELF.

Bear facts

Paws don't come any bigger than those of bears. A grizzly has dinner-plate-sized paws with claws that are longer than human fingers. The bear uses these all-purpose tools to dig marmots and other rodents from their dens, scoop fish from rivers, and slash at larger prey such as moose.

The polar bear prefers bashing to slashing. Each of its massive forelegs ends in an 40-lb (18-kg) paw. When hungry, a polar bear waits beside a seal's breathing hole in the ice. Eventually, the seal bobs up for air and—wallop!—it's dispatched with a single blow. The bear can also use a paw like a meat hook, jabbing the claws into a seal to haul it out of the water, before crushing its skull with a bite to the head.

Pincer movement

Far smaller than a bear's claws, but equally destructive in their watery world, are the pincers of

THE SPINES ON A PRAYING MANTIS'S FRONT LEGS HOLD VICTIMS IN A VISE-LIKE GRIP AS THE MANTIS DEVOURS THEM ALIVE.

crustaceans such as lobsters and crabs. These are a pair of modified front legs that serve both as prey catchers and as defensive weapons. Just as mammals have specialized teeth, lobsters have specialized claws. The larger, heavier pincer crushes shellfish such as mussels and clams, while the smaller, lighter claw has saw-like edges to tear and shred soft prey such as worms.

Praying mantises and some other insects have a specially adapted pair of pincerlike front legs. Each leg is jointed in such a way that it can fold back on itself to trap prey. Interlocking spines on the inner edge of the legs impale the victim as the "pincers" close, holding it tight and making escape impossible.

S inister suckers

The eight muscular, flexible "arms" of an octopus don't have claws or pincers,

but they've got something just as good—suction pads. The long arms investigate crevices and cracks in rocks in search of prey. When the octopus finds something edible, the suckers hold the creature tight,

THE COMMON LOBSTER USES ITS TWO LARGE PINCERS TO GET AT THE TASTY FLESH OF SHELLFISH—AND GIVE ATTACKERS A NASTY NIP.

but they're a reality in the animal world. Frogs and toads use their long, sticky tongues to catch live prey and haul it back into the mouth. It's a neat trick, but the giant anteater beats it hands (or tongues) down. The giant anteater's tongue can measure a massive 24 in (62 cm) long, and is covered in tiny spines and coated with gooey saliva to trap termites and ants. The anteater splits open their nests with its claws and probes the tunnels and chambers with its tongue. Flicking in and out up to 150 times a minute, the tongue can mop up about 30,000 insects per day!

preventing it from struggling as the octopus starts to feed.

As well as eight arms lined with suckers, cuttlefish and squid have two longer, sucker-tipped tentacles, which shoot out in just 0.01 seconds to clasp swimming prey. The tentacles reel in their catch, which is smothered by the arms and torn apart by the parrot-like "beak."

S ticky flickers
"Killer tongues" may sound like the title of a horror movie,

Breathtaking boas

Boas and pythons are known as constrictors. These snakes use a weapon that literally takes their victim's breath away—it's their whole body! A constrictor loops a few coils around its prey and grips it firmly. Each time the prey breathes out, the coils tighten a little more. The prey's rib cage can't expand to take in fresh air, so the animal gradually suffocates. Then the snake engulfs the animal with its jaws, which dislocate to let the mouth gape as wide as possible. With the snake's throat stretched to the limit by its dinner, waves of muscle contractions force the prey down into the stomach.

THIS ANACONDA HAS KILLED A CAIMAN BY CONSTRICTION. SUCH LARGE PREY CAN TAKE UP TO AN HOUR TO SWALLOW AND PERHAPS A WEEK TO DIGEST.

Large constrictors can tackle sizeable prey. For example, the anaconda—the world's heaviest snake, weighing up to 485 lb (220 kg)—can devour a caiman 6.5 ft (2 m) long. After such a big meal, the snake may not eat again for 12 months, and yet still stay perfectly healthy.

Not surprisingly, when a large constrictor does make a catch, every last bit of the animal is consumed. If you had to wait a year for your next meal, would you leave any scraps on your plate?

35

HUNTING STRATEGIES

E very predator needs a hunting strategy. Some rely on speed and power in the chase to make a kill. Others prefer to stalk prey, pouncing when they get close enough. Many simply sit and wait, motionless and concealed, ready to strike at unsuspecting creatures that venture near. Whatever the strategy, the slightest miscalculation can result in a missed meal, wasted effort, and an empty belly!

S peed kills

What can go from 0–60 mph (0–96 km/h) in 3 seconds? Is it a sports car or a superbike? No, it's the cheetah—a high-speed predator that lives on Africa's grasslands. This cat is the world's fastest land animal, and it has such an amazing sprint that it can outrun every other grassland animal.

When the cheetah gets within sprinting range of prey such as gazelles and impala, its long, powerful legs launch it into action with an explosive burst of speed. The cheetah's extremely flexible hips, shoulders, and

THE LONG TAIL STEADIES THE CHEETAH AS IT MAKES TIGHT TURNS FOLLOWING THE ZIGZAGGING RUNS OF ITS PREY.

spine allow its legs to cover 23 ft (7 m) with each stride. Like the spikes on an athlete's shoes, its semiretractable claws give its feet extra grip, while grooves on its footpads act like the tread on car tires to aid braking and avoid skidding.

Closing in on the fleeing prey, the cheetah trips up the animal with a neat flick from its paw, sending the victim crashing to the ground. The chase is usually over in less than 20 seconds. The cheetah quickly clamps its jaws around the windpipe of the stunned prey, and suffocates it.

The cheetah is built for speed, but it has little stamina. If it hasn't caught its prey after about 440 yards (400 m), it gives up the chase. By then, its energy reserves have been used up, and it is in danger of overheating. The cheetah has to rest and cool down for up to 30 minutes before trying again.

Tiny tiger

No matter how large or small a predator is, speed can always give it the edge over its prey. Tiger beetles are the sprint champions of the insect world. These six-legged stars can cover

WEIRD WORLD

DURING A CHASE, A CHEETAH'S BODY TEMPERATURE MAY RISE TO 105°F (40°C). IF IT WERE TO KEEP SPRINTING FOR ABOUT A MINUTE, THIS COULD CAUSE BRAIN DAMAGE.

THE FORCE OF A PEREGRINE'S
STRIKE CAN DECAPITATE ITS PREY

up to 3.3 ft (1 m) per second, which works out at 2.2 mph (3.6 km/h). A tiger beetle lives in a burrow, from where it makes well-timed dashes to run down ants, grasshoppers, and other beetles. Death comes swiftly in the form of the killer's savage, sickle-shaped jaws, which swing into action to slice up the prey.

The fastest flying insects are dragonflies. They cruise up and down rivers at 30 mph (50 km/h), plucking prey from the air. But these air aces have even faster enemies—young peregrine falcons, which use dragonflies to hone their own hunting skills to perfection.

HIGH-SPEED DIVES ARE CRUCIAL TO THE PEREGRINE'S SUCCESS AS A PREDATOR—IN LEVEL FLIGHT, IT CAN RARELY CATCH UP WITH FAST-FLYING BIRDS SUCH AS PIGEONS.

Aerial interceptor

The peregrine falcon is quite simply the fastest creature on Earth, and it uses its incredible speed to make midair strikes on other birds from high altitude.

Once its eyes have locked on to a target—let's say a pigeon— the falcon attacks. The wings fold back and the tail closes to give it a sleek, bulletlike shape. Then it plummets downward in a steep dive at up to 125 mph (200 km/h). As it zeros in on its prey, muscles continually adjust the curve of its eyeballs to keep its target in focus. Impact! The peregrine's talons rip into the pigeon and break its spine.

If the peregrine overshoots the target, it can pull out of the dive and then zoom back up to hit the prey from below. Pulling out of such a dive puts the falcon's body under immense stress. It's a mystery how the peregrine can do this without losing consciousness or injuring itself.

A irbags and crash helmets

Other daredevils of the skies include blue-footed boobies. These high-rise anglers launch themselves like guided missiles from a height of about 100 ft (30 m) to attack shoals of fish below the waves. Although they don't reach such high speeds as the peregrine, hitting the water at 60 mph (96 km/h) can hurt like crazy. That's why they have built-in "airbags" and "crash helmets" to protect them. Before the dive, the birds gulp air to inflate special sacs in the neck and breast that help to cushion the blow. Boobies also have an extra-strong skull, so that they can emerge from the dive without a throbbing headache!

LOG ON...
Cracking crocs at www.
pbs.org/wgbh/nova/crocs/

LIKE A SQUADRON OF DIVE-BOMBERS, A FLOCK OF BLUE-FOOTED BOOBIES ATTACKS A SHOAL OF FISH IN THE PACIFIC OCEAN.

SECURED BY SILK SAFETY LINES, A JUMPING SPIDER PROPELS ITSELF INTO THE AIR.

Stealthy stalkers

Not every predator is designed for high-speed chases and dives, and many are better suited to stalking prey—sneaking up unnoticed and then making a leap or a quick dash to finish the job. Surprise, rather than speed, is the key ingredient.

Cats are especially skilled at stalking, and have spongy footpads to muffle their sound as they approach prey.

A stalking cat keeps its body as close to the ground as possible to avoid detection. If the prey glances toward it, the cat freezes in place, its muscles taut, and holds the pose until the animal looks away. Then the cat resumes its stalk, gradually edging to within striking distance of its prey.

Like cats, jumping spiders are also stalkers. A jumping spider's eyes can spot prey such as a fly from up to 12 in (30 cm) away. Having crept to within jumping range, the spider attaches silk safety lines to a surface, so that it won't fall far if its jump isn't successful. A sudden increase in blood pressure extends the rear

A CHAMELEON'S TONGUE CAN BE LONGER THAN ITS BODY. THE LIZARD'S AIM MUST BE PERFECT, BECAUSE ONCE THE TONGUE IS LAUNCHED, ITS DIRECTION CAN'T BE CHANGED.

WEIRD WORLD

A CHAMELEON'S EYES CAN MOVE INDEPENDENTLY, SO IT CAN SEE IN TWO DIRECTIONS AT ONCE. WHEN HUNTING, ONE EYE WATCHES OUT FOR DANGER, WHILE THE OTHER LOOKS FOR PREY.

legs like tiny pistons, hurling the spider through the air—perhaps by as much as 40 times its own body length. The spider lands on the fly and uses its sturdy front legs to pin the victim down. Then the spider's fangs go about their deadly work.

L unging jaws

Nile crocodiles do their stalking underwater. In Africa's dry season, the lack of fresh water forces mammals such as zebras and wildebeest to drink at places where crocodiles lurk. Lying low and unseen in the water, with just its eyes, nostrils, and ears breaking the surface, a crocodile selects a victim from the animals crowded at the water's edge. Then it sinks down and paddles as close to the shore as it can. With a sudden thrust from its powerful hind legs or its massive tail, the crocodile bursts out of the water. The huge jaws may slam shut on the victim, or the crocodile may stun the animal with a hammer

blow from its huge head. The prey is then dragged into the water, where it's drowned and eaten.

R eptile sharpshooter

If you can't leap or lunge, you may need an extra something to help you catch your prey once you've stalked it. For lizards called chameleons, it's a long, whiplash tongue that can strike with lightning-fast speed. The tongue, which is rolled up inside the mouth when not in use, is covered in sticky mucus and has a suction cup on the end.

A NILE CROCODILE LUNGES AT A DRINKING WILDEBEEST. IT USUALLY GRABS PREY BY THE MUZZLE, BUT ANY BODY PART WILL DO.

When prey is spotted, spiral muscles inside the tongue contract widthways, shooting out the tongue at up to 16.5 ft (5 m) per second, rather like squeezing a wet bar of soap from your hand. Accelerating up to five times faster than a jet fighter, the tongue hits the target like a glue-tipped dart.

THERE'S NO ESCAPE FOR THIS MOUSE FROM THE JAWS OF AN ORNATE HORNED FROG.

Bull's-eye! A different set of muscles reels the tongue back in again, and the prey is then crushed between the bony jaws.

All mouth

Sit-and-wait predators don't actively seek food—they wait for food to come to them. The ornate horned frog has the ambush game down to a fine

art. This forest dweller pushes its bulky body so far under the leaf litter that only its eyes protrude. And there it waits— silent but perfectly alert—until a mouse, lizard, bird, or insect strays too close. In a flash, the jaws open and shut around the prey with a loud snap.

The width of the mouth can be more than half the length of the frog's body—wide enough to swallow a rat whole. In fact, the ornate horned frog is such a glutton that it will gulp down virtually anything that fits in its voluminous mouth! The frog has such a compulsion to feed that it can't resist swallowing distasteful prey, even if it means spitting out an unpleasant meal later.

Fast food

To find the ultimate in rapid reactions, check out the frogfish. Its warty skin provides it with camouflage as it skulks around coral reefs snatching prey with movements way too fast for the human eye to see. As a victim approaches, the fish opens its mouth, which rapidly expands to 12 times its normal volume, sucking the creature to its doom. There's no time for the prey to feel startled,

DESPITE ITS MONSTROUS SIZE, THE WHALE SHARK IS HARMLESS TO HUMANS.

because it's all over
in 0.006 seconds—
perhaps the fastest
movement in the
animal world.

Nature's trawlers

Whale sharks and basking
sharks, the two largest fish in
the world, also find that having
a big mouth is an asset. But they
don't have rapid reactions like
the frogfish—because they don't
need them. These gentle giants
feed like underwater trawlers.
The sharks cruise along slowly
with jaws agape, guzzling vast
quantities of seawater,
which they then squeeze
out through their gills.
Special filters in the gills strain
out small fish, shrimplike
crustaceans called krill, and
other tiny creatures.

So you see, hunting isn't just
about rushing around getting
hot and tired. Sometimes it can
be a laid-back, leisurely affair!

HIDE AND SEEK

In the battle of wits between predator and prey, the key to success is to stay out of sight. Camouflage is the way that an animal's color, pattern, and shape help it to blend in with its surroundings, rendering it either hard to spot or even invisible unless it moves. Camouflage can conceal predators until the final moment of attack, and hide prey from the bloodthirsty gaze of would-be killers.

Color and pattern

A green vine snake can lie unnoticed among the lush foliage of the rain forest, while a polar bear's white coat helps it to blend in with the Arctic landscape of snow and ice. But plain colors are rarely enough to hide animals well, because most habitats contain a range of colors and varying amounts of light and shadow. So a camouflage that's patterned with spots, stripes, blotches, or other shapes tends to be more effective. The spots of leopards and jaguars, for example, help to conceal the

WHEN ZEBRAS STAND IN A HERD, THEIR BOLD STRIPES SEEM TO RUN INTO EACH OTHER, BLURRING THE BODY SHAPES OF THE ANIMALS.

WITH ITS SPOTTED COAT, THIS LEOPARD
LOOKS LIKE PART OF THE SCENERY.

animals both in open expanses
of long grass and in the
dappled light of the forest.

Patterns can also make an
animal's outline less distinct.
That's how zebras' stripes work.
A predator looking at a herd of
zebras is faced with a confusing
mass of stripes. The hunter
finds it difficult to select prey
because it can't pick out the
shape of an individual animal.

Counter-shading

In the open sea, where there's
nothing to hide animals from
the eyes of predator or prey,
many ocean creatures use a sort
of two-tone camouflage called
counter-shading. Most fish, for
example, have dark upper
surfaces, and whitish
undersides. When looked
at from above, by

birds with rumbling tummies,
their dark backs merge with the
murky depths of the water
below, making the fish difficult
to spot. When viewed from
below, by hungry deep-sea
predators, their bright bellies
blend in with the well-lit
surface water.

> ### WEIRD WORLD
> THE THREE-TOED SLOTH
> CLEANS ITSELF SO RARELY AND
> MOLTS SO SLOWLY THAT
> ALGAE (TINY PLANTS) GROW IN
> ITS HAIR AND TURN IT GREEN,
> HELPING IT TO BLEND INTO
> THE RAINFOREST OF CENTRAL
> AMERICA.

Try a disguise

For vulnerable animals, both on land and at sea, one of the best ways to avoid being eaten is to use color and shape to disguise themselves as inedible objects. Insects are especially good at this. There are bugs with

THE WOBBEGONG'S CAMOUFLAGE DISGUISES ITS TRUE, DEATH-DEALING IDENTITY.

spiky projections on their backs that resemble thorns, thin stick insects that are indistinguishable from twigs, and caterpillars and weevils that are the spitting image of bird droppings—yuck!

Predators, too, can play at this game. Australia's wobbegong shark has a flat, mottled body, and skin tassels on its head that look like seaweed fronds. These features work together like an invisibility cloak, making the shark disappear among the rocks of the seafloor. For its prey, the shark just isn't there— that is, until it strikes!

TWO GREEN LEAF INSECTS FEED ON A TWIG. IT'S DIFFICULT TO TELL THE FOLIAGE AND THE INSECTS APART.

Snappy dressers

If you can't blend in with the background, try wearing it! The decorator crab covers itself with seaweed and marine animals such as sponges. These plants and animals continue to grow, forming a kind of living suit that hides the crab from view.

summer, the fox begins to grow a new white coat again.

Color changers

Chameleons have color-changing down to a fine art. They can match the color of their background by expanding or contracting special pigment-containing skin cells called chromatophores.

THE DECORATOR CRAB HAS TINY HOOKS ON ITS BODY, TO WHICH IT ATTACHES MATERIAL FROM THE SEABED.

But when the crab moves to a different place to feed, it has to discard the old suit and make another one using materials from its new surroundings.

The Arctic fox prefers a fur coat to a suit, but it too needs a regular change of "clothing." In summer, when the snow and ice melt in the lands near the North Pole, the fox sheds its white winter coat and replaces it with a covering of grayish-brown fur that camouflages it against the bare landscape. Near the end of

Chameleons can also lighten or darken their skin to match changing levels of daylight, and even put on displays of bright colors to ward off rivals and impress potential mates.

SITTING ON FLOWERS, CRAB SPIDERS GRAB INSECTS THAT COME TO SIP NECTAR.

In each case, the color changes take just a few minutes to complete. For crab spiders, which hide on flowers and prey on insects, color changing takes a lot longer. The spiders adopt the color of the flower on which they've chosen to hide. But when they're placed on a flower of another color, it can take up to two days for their chromatophores to adjust to the new color. Until then, they stick out like a sore thumb!

Octopuses have the fastest-changing chromatophores of all. As they move over different surfaces, these ocean artists can produce eye-popping color changes in a fraction of a second. They can also alter their texture to help them blend in even more, making their skin knobbly and rough to roam over rocks or coral reefs, and smoothing it out when they encounter flat sand.

Marvelous mimics

Not all animals try to hide. Some, such as tropical lionfish and South American poison-dart frogs, use their colors to draw attention to themselves. These animals are usually poisonous or unpleasant-tasting, or able to dish out a painful defensive sting. They have patterns of vivid, contrasting colors that say "Keep away! I'm dangerous!" to other animals. The most common warning colors are yellow, orange, red, and black. Some predators instinctively know that

A POISON-DART FROG'S SKIN CONTAINS TOXIC CHEMICALS. PREDATORS IGNORE ITS WARNING COLORS AT THEIR PERIL.

they should avoid animals clad in these colors—others quickly learn after a bad experience with boldly patterned prey.

Warning colors are such a successful way of staying off a predator's menu that harmless animals sometimes mimic them. Non-venomous milksnakes in

viper. When threatened, the caterpillar waves its rear end in the air. This is shaped like a snake's head and has facelike markings, complete with false eyes. As the tiny "viper" rears up at them, predators beat a hasty retreat—after all, who wants to be bitten by their own dinner?

HOVERFLIES COPY THE COLORS OF WASPS, BUT DON'T HAVE STINGERS

the southern US mimic the red-black-and-yellow bands of deadly coral snakes. The colorful hoax fools many predators into thinking that the milksnakes also carry a lethal bite.

Many mimics can also imitate the way dangerous animals behave. One Malaysian stick insect arches its abdomen over its head to make itself look like an angry scorpion. Similarly, some spiders pretend to be ants, waving their front legs around as though they were antennae. Birds wary of ant stings give the spiders a wide berth!

There is even a Costa Rican hawkmoth caterpillar that impersonates a venomous

A HARMLESS MILKSNAKE HAS THE SAME BANDS OF COLOR AS A DEADLY CORAL SNAKE, BUT IN A DIFFERENT ORDER.

49

WORKING TOGETHER

A job is always easier when someone else lends a hand, and life is no different in the world of predators. Working as a team enables some predators to hunt more efficiently, or to catch larger animals than they could alone, giving them a wider choice of prey. Other animals hunt in swarms, not making coordinated attacks but using sheer numbers to swamp their victims.

Pack hunters

As the golden glow of dawn lights up the horizon, a pack of African wild dogs sets out across the grassy plains at a slow trot. This is a hunting party, and before mid-morning they will be gorging themselves on flesh and blood.

African wild dogs have incredible stamina. These long-distance runners can chase large mammals, such as gazelles, wildebeest, antelopes, and zebras, until their

The dogs devour the body as swiftly as possible to prevent other predators from stealing their hard-earned food. For such savage killers, the dogs seem almost polite as they feed at the carcass. The whole pack shares the kill, with youngsters being encouraged to take their fill first.

IN PURSUIT OF PREY, AFRICAN WILD DOGS CAN MAINTAIN A SPEED OF 25 MPH (40 KM/H) FOR 3 MILES (5 KM) OR MORE.

prey simply can't go on. During the hunt, the dogs work like a relay team, each taking turn to lead the chase, which can last for hours. As the prey tires and slows, the lead dog may grab the animal's tail to try to halt its progress. Then the dogs close in to nip at the animal's belly and rump. Assailed from all sides, the prey is quickly disemboweled—often while it's still on its feet! It's a gruesome death, but it's usually over in a matter of seconds.

Family matters

African wild dogs, along with wolves, lions, and spotted hyenas, are "social" animals, which means that they live in family groups. Individuals may catch small animals, but by hunting as a group and coordinating their efforts, they can tackle prey much larger than themselves. For example, with many sets of jaws and claws to attack their victim, a pack of gray wolves can bring down a moose, reindeer, or musk ox up to 10 times the weight of a single wolf.

On the run

Hunting large mammals can be dangerous work. A kick from a hoof can crack a skull, while horns and antlers can

A WILDEBEEST CAN FEND OFF A LONE HUNTING DOG, BUT IT IS SIMPLY OVERWHELMED BY A MASSED ATTACK FROM AN ENTIRE PACK.

gore deep wounds. The key to a successful hunt is to get the prey moving. Once an animal is running, it's more vulnerable and less able to strike out at its attackers. To make things easier,

HUNTING AS A GROUP HELPS TO STRENGTHEN THE SOCIAL BONDS BETWEEN THE MEMBERS OF A WOLF PACK.

predators target young, sick, or old animals, which are slower and unlikely to fight back.

In a grazing herd, the weaker animals may hide behind the stronger ones for protection. The challenge for predators is to panic the herd into stampeding, so that they can separate the weak from the strong.

S eparate and slay

African wild dogs do this by simply running toward a herd. Because of their speed and incredible stamina, they don't care if their prey sees them. The message seems to be, "You can run, but we'll get you in the end!" And they usually do—more than 80 percent of hunts are successful, making them the most efficient of all the large carnivores. Wolves and lions aren't so quick in the chase, so they need to sneak up close before they reveal themselves. Their prey may be able to outrun them if it gets enough of a head start.

L ionesses at work

In a group, or "pride," of lions, it's usually females that find food (the males' role is to defend the pride). When the lionesses hunt, they often spread out and encircle a

THESE LIONESSES ARE EATING A BUFFALO. MALES OFTEN MUSCLE IN TO GET THE BEST BITS OF THE CARCASS. THE CUBS EAT LAST, SO IF FOOD IS SCARCE, THEY GO HUNGRY.

herd of prey, crouching low to keep out of sight. Once in position, a few of the lionesses stand up to attract attention. If all goes to plan, the herd starts to flee—straight toward the other lionesses, which spring the ambush. The hunters work together to separate an animal from the rest of the herd. Then one of the ambushers leaps on its back and drags it to the ground. Small victims are killed with a bite to the back of the neck to sever the spinal cord. Larger ones are suffocated by a bite to the throat.

Ape attack

Group hunting is also practiced by some African primates. Male baboons occasionally cooperate to stalk and chase prey, and then share the meat after the kill. But the most sophisticated group hunting of all is carried out by chimpanzees, with red colobus monkeys

AN OLIVE BABOON CARRIES THE REMAINS OF A YOUNG GAZELLE.

to turn back—right into the clutches of the pursuing chimps.

Herding fish

While land predators cooperate to split up herds, in the ocean orcas and dolphins use team-work to herd fish into neat, compact shoals to make feeding easier. Called "fish balling," it ensures that the hunters get more fish per mouthful.

Bottlenose dolphins have been known to chase fish toward mudbanks, creating a swell of water that washes the fish onto the mud. The dolphins beach themselves and gobble up as many fish as they can, before slipping back into the sea.

Orcas have a range of group-hunting strategies. Occasionally, a group, or "pod," of orcas will work together to attack large prey such as a gray or blue whale calf.

as their favorite prey. When an all-male hunting party spies a troop of colobuses in the forest canopy, one chimp, the "driver," climbs into the trees to get the monkeys moving. Other chimps, called "chasers," pursue the colobuses, while "flankers" take up positions on either side to cut off their escape routes. The "ambusher" rushes ahead of the fleeing monkeys and hides. He springs out when they get near, causing the startled colobuses

They tirelessly harass mother and calf until they can separate the pair and move in for the kill. At other times they go "penguin-tipping," with some orcas flipping up ice floes to tip sleeping penguins into the mouths of other pod members.

B ubble-netting

Blowing bubbles can be fun for us, but for humpback whales it's an ingenious way of feeding. As they circle a shoal of fish from below, the whales force a continuous stream of air bubbles out of their blowholes. The rising bubble streams create a spiral wall that the fish can't escape from. Trapped by this "bubble net," the fish can only swim upward. Eventually, they find themselves splashing and leaping at the surface, with nowhere to go. The whales then surge up through the center of the bubble net, open-mouthed, and gulp down fish by the thousand.

LOG ON...
www.szgdocent.org/
aa/a-wildog.htm

UP TO 24 HUMPBACKS MAY JOIN TOGETHER WHEN BUBBLE-NETTING. FISH ARE SIEVED FROM THE WATER BY COMBLIKE BALEEN PLATES THAT HANG FROM THE WHALE'S UPPER JAW.

P iranha peril

Some predators hunt in such big groups that they can simply overwhelm their victims. It's not a coordinated strike, but the victim finds that there are far too many attackers to fight back. by scores of fish, each one able to carve out a walnut-sized piece of flesh...well, you've had it!

Despite their reputation, many of the 26 piranha species are herbivores, feeding on seeds and aquatic plants. Even flesh-eating

A PIRANHA SHOAL CAN REDUCE A DEER TO A SKELETON IN MINUTES

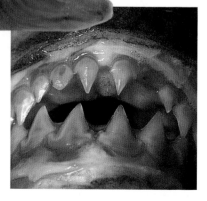

piranhas, such as red-bellies, rarely attack strong, healthy animals swimming in the water. It's usually only the flailing of drowning or weak animals that gets their stomachs rumbling, or the scent of blood

MEASURING 14 IN (36 CM) LONG, WITH THICK-SET JAWS AND RAZOR-SHARP TEETH, THE RED-BELLIED PIRANHA IS A FISH TO BE AVOIDED!

The flesh-eating piranha fish found in South American rivers are the most notorious example of this. Other fish are their usual prey, but given the chance they'll devour animals as large as deer, horses, or even humans. When a piranha shoal gets a hint of a meal, they can't help nibbling. And when you're being nibbled

seeping from a wound. First, a few wary fish take "sample" bites from the prey to test its fighting spirit. Then the rest of the shoal piles in to nip away at the body. The water boils with thrashing fish, in a frenzy of snapping jaws. Soon there's nothing left but bones!

Irresistible swarm

An army of a million troops is not to be messed with—even if it's made up of ants! Army ants don't make permanent homes. Instead, the ants cling to each other's bodies to form a temporary "living nest," with the queen at its center. Each day the army sends out vast foraging columns up to 65 ft (20 m) across. Any insects and spiders in the path of their relentless advance are killed and then dismembered—up to 100,000 of them daily. They can even overcome snakes, and have been known to kill human babies left unattended.

This type of hunting isn't the result of deliberate teamwork. Each ant is just obeying a few simple rules of behavior. But the combined effect makes the swarm of marauding ants seem like a single organism— a kind of super-predator.

ARMY ANTS IMMOBILIZE PREY WITH THEIR STINGERS, CHOP IT UP WITH THEIR JAWS, AND CARRY IT OFF TO THE "NEST."

VENOMOUS VILLAINS

When some predators kill, it's not a gory bloodbath, just a quick, neat injection of a poisonous fluid called venom. These hunters know all about the sinister art of poisoning, and they use it to kill prey without risking injury in a long battle. Like working as a team, injecting prey with venom can also allow a predator to conquer animals much larger than itself—except in this case, it doesn't have to share the spoils!

Vicious venom

Venom is a cocktail of harmful chemicals produced by glands in an animal's body. There are two main types of venom. One type damages the nervous system, paralyzing a victim or stopping its heart or lungs from working. The other type attacks the blood system, damaging red blood cells and causing uncontrollable bleeding or blood clotting. Venom may also contain enzymes—substances that start to dissolve the prey's innards before it's consumed.

For venom to be effective, a predator needs to get it inside the body of its prey. Venomous snakes do this using specialized teeth called fangs. In some snakes, the fangs are at the front of the mouth, in others they're at the rear.

A VENOM DROPLET GLISTENS ON THE FANG OF THIS AFRICAN PUFF ADDER, A MEMBER OF THE VIPER FAMILY.

Injectors and chewers

Front-fanged snakes have thin, backward-curving fangs in their upper jaw. The fangs are hollow and connect to a pair of venom glands in the head. When the fangs puncture the victim's flesh, muscles squeeze the glands to pump venom into the wound. The system works like the hypodermic needles that doctors use— except that these injections don't cure, they kill!

Cobras, mambas, taipans, and sea snakes have fixed front fangs that are always ready to dish out a stabbing bite. Vipers and pit vipers have hinged front fangs that fold back out of the way when not required. They swing down and lock into biting position as the snake opens its jaws wide to strike. To avoid damaging the fangs, the snake withdraws them immediately after biting.

Rear-fanged snakes have shorter, grooved fangs. When the snake bites, venom just trickles down the grooves and into the wound. Rear-fanged snakes

often bite repeatedly, using a "chewing" action to work the venom into the flesh.

Germ-carrying jaws

The only other reptiles that use venom are two lizards—the Mexican beaded lizard and the Gila monster, both of the southern US and Mexico. Like rear-fanged snakes, they have grooved teeth for channeling toxins into prey, although theirs are on the lower jaw, not the upper one. Shrews, the only mammals that hunt with venom, also use poison-channeling teeth to trickle in the toxins.

The Komodo dragon, a relative of the Gila monster and beaded lizard, doesn't possess venom,

THE KOMODO DRAGON'S BACTERIA-LADEN SALIVA HELPS IT TO BRING DOWN WILD BOAR AND OTHER LARGE ANIMALS.

but its saliva can be equally effective on anything it bites. This lumbering giant, which is found on only a few Indonesian islands, is the world's largest lizard. It mostly eats carrion, but it will take live prey given the chance. Too slow to run animals down, the Komodo usually ambushes its prey with a lunging bite. Should the victim escape, it's unlikely to get far. The lizard's saliva is so full of harmful bacteria that the wound rapidly becomes infected, and the animal soon crumples to the ground. Flicking its tongue in and out, the lizard follows the animal's scent trail until it tracks down the collapsed victim. Then it begins to feast.

WEIRD WORLD

THE BITE OF A FEW SPIDERS CAN CAUSE HUMAN FLESH TO DIE. THIS "NECROSIS" WAS ONCE ASSUMED TO BE AN EFFECT OF THE SPIDERS' VENOM, BUT SCIENTISTS NOW BELIEVE THAT IT'S PRODUCED BY BACTERIA ON THEIR FANGS.

E ight-legged exterminators
In contrast to lizards, all spiders can deliver a poisonous bite, squeezing venom out of the tooth-like

fangs on their main mouthparts, called chelicerae. Spider venom, like the venom of all predators that poison by biting, started out as digestive juices. Over millions of years, it developed into a complex mixture of toxic chemicals and tissue-destroying enzymes. Spiders have soft bodies that are easily damaged, and they aren't equipped with grasping claws for restraining prey. Spider venom is designed to be fast-acting, so that prey is subdued quickly and doesn't get the chance to injure the spider.

Bird-eaters and spider-killers

Among the biggest and most fearsome-looking spiders are the bird-eating, or tarantula, spiders of the Americas. With large, well-stocked poison glands, long fangs, and leg-spans of up to 11 in (28 cm) these hairy monsters don't hesitate to take on large prey such as birds, lizards, frogs, mice, and even venomous snakes.

Despite being so well-armed, the bird-eaters frequently fall victim to female spider-hunting wasps. It may seem crazy to challenge such a big spider to a duel, but it's a contest that the wasp almost always wins, thanks to the poison-packed stinger at the end of its abdomen. After a brief tussle and a jab from the stinger, the defeated spider is left helpless and paralyzed.

LOG ON...
www.exn.ca/snakes/
for slithery snake facts

THE GOLIATH TARANTULA OF SOUTH AMERICA HAS THE BIGGEST FANGS OF ANY SPIDER, MEASURING UP TO 0.5 IN (12 MM) LONG.

A COSTA RICAN SPIDER-HUNTING WASP DRAGS A CAPTURED SPIDER TO ITS BURROW.

The twist to the story is that the wasp doesn't eat her prey—she's strictly vegetarian, feeding on flower nectar and pollen. She only catches spiders to feed to her meat-loving offspring.

Having made a catch, the wasp digs a burrow, into which she drags the helpless spider. Then she lays an egg on the spider, seals up the burrow, and flies off. Unable to move but still alive, the spider becomes the food supply—a kind of living pantry—for the young wasp larva that hatches from the egg. When the larva changes into an adult, it gives up its carnivorous ways and becomes a plant-feeder, just like its mother.

More stingers

Wasps aren't the only hunters armed with stingers. Many ant species also possess a stinger at the end of the abdomen, which injects an acidic venom into prey. (Wasp stings are alkaline.) The sting of the Costa Rican bullet ant, for example, is so painful that it feels as if you've been shot, while as few as 30 stings from Australia's bulldog ant are enough to send humans to an early grave.

Not all ant stings need to pack such a punch. It's often not the power of the sting that counts, but how many times you're stung. Fire ants only have a mild sting, but they attack in vast numbers and deliver such a bombardment of stings that the effect on prey is deadly.

THE SCORPION SUBDUES SMALL OR
DEFENSELESS PREY, SUCH AS
GRASSHOPPERS, WITH ITS
PINCERS. BUT AGAINST
STRONG OR WELL-ARMED
OPPONENTS, IT USES ITS
STINGER AS WELL.

REMAINS OF
GRASSHOPPER

Another invertebrate
that's a venomous villain is
the scorpion. The bulb-shaped
tip of its long abdomen consists
of a stinger and a venom gland
surrounded by muscles. The
scorpion strikes by arching its
abdomen over its head and
repeatedly stabbing the stinger
into the victim. With each stab,
the muscles force venom into
the prey's body, so that the
creature is soon out of action.

TIGER CENTIPEDES OF SOUTHEAST ASIA GET
THEIR NAME FROM THEIR COLORFUL
MARKINGS AND THEIR FIERCE,
CARNIVOROUS HABITS.

Lethal legs
A venom-delivery
system doesn't have to
be in a predator's head or at the
end of its abdomen. In the case
of centipedes, it's in the legs.
A centipede has at least 30 legs,
but two of them in particular
can mean big trouble for prey.
The front pair, on either side of
the mouth, are modified into
hooklike claws. In the base of
each claw is a venom gland that
connects to a
small opening

near the claw's tip. Big tropical centipedes, some up to 13 in (33 cm) long, use these claws to grab, jab, and inject locusts, cockroaches, and small reptiles.

Commotion in the ocean
There are poison perils lurking below the waves, too. Squid, octopuses, and cuttlefish may look comical, but their saliva is laced with strong nerve poisons that quickly overcome their prey. In fact, the venom of the blue-ringed octopus is such a potent potion that it can kill a person. So be warned, looks can be deceptive...as can size.

Cone shells are slow-moving ocean predators no more than

SOME JELLYFISH TENTACLES ARE MORE THAN 100 FT (30 M) LONG

1.6 in (4 cm) long. Despite their size and speed, they are expert hunters of fish, worms, and mollusks. A cone shell has modified teeth, located on a mouthpart called a radula, that can be fired from its mouth like harpoons. When a tooth strikes home, the cone shell injects venom through the tooth's hollow shaft. A thread links the tooth to the radula, so the cone shell winds in its paralyzed prey, like an angler reeling in fish.

Deadly danglers
Cone shells are armed with a dozen or so toxic harpoons, but that's nothing compared to jellyfish, whose dangling

SEA NETTLE JELLYFISH OFTEN INFLICT PAINFUL STINGS ON SWIMMERS.

ANEMONES LOOK LIKE FLOWERS, BUT THEY ARE REALLY DEADLY PREDATORS, AS THIS SHRIMP HAS DISCOVERED.

tentacles are equipped with thousands or even millions of exploding stingers called nematocysts. Each stinger contains a poison-filled thread with a flesh-piercing barb at its tip. When triggered by touch or by chemicals in the water, the nematocysts fire their poison darts into nearby prey, such as fish or crustaceans.

Nematocysts are formidable weapons, but to some marine turtles, including the hawksbill, the presence of a jellyfish doesn't say "Danger!" but "Party time!" These turtles are immune to nematocyst venom, and they like nothing better than to dig into a big portion of jelly!

Cnidarian cousins

Jellyfish belong to a group of animals called cnidarians, which also includes anemones. These, too, use stinging tentacles to catch prey. Anemones can't swim or float like jellyfish, but spend their lives glued to rocks or other objects, waving their tentacles around in the water above. If animals swim into the mass of tentacles, they're stung and pulled down into the anemone's waiting mouth.

Whether it's delivered by tentacles, harpoons, stingers, or fangs, venom is highly efficient at dispatching prey with as little fuss and mess as possible.

WEIRD WORLD

SOME HERMIT CRABS ATTACH ANEMONES TO THEIR SHELLS TO WARD OFF PREDATORS. THE ANEMONES ALSO BENEFIT, BECAUSE THEY REGULARLY GET MOVED TO NEW FEEDING GROUNDS.

AMAZING ATTACKERS

When predators set out to catch prey, they use every means they can to guarantee a high success rate. This can involve making traps, such as sticky webs and steep pits, firing missiles at victims, zapping prey with sound blasts and electric shocks, and even hypnotizing them. From traps to trickery, anything's allowed in the killing game!

Top traps

Have you ever walked right into a spiderweb without realizing it was there, then shuddered with disgust as you brushed off the clingy threads? Consider yourself lucky—when an insect flies headlong into a spiderweb, it faces certain death!

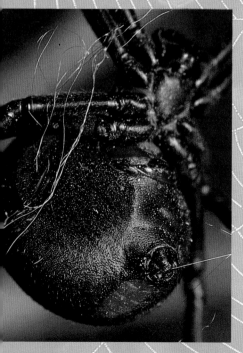

Incredibly strong, amazingly lightweight, very stretchy, and almost invisible, spiderwebs are the most awesome traps made by any animal. They're made of a special material called silk, which is a form of liquid protein produced by glands in a spider's abdomen. Drawn out by the spider's legs, the silk emerges from tubes called spinnerets and hardens as soon as it comes in contact with the air.

Expert engineers

Spiders spin numerous different types of web, using a mixture of dry and sticky silk threads. Many webs are flat, like a

YOU CAN SEE THE SILK EMERGING FROM THE SPINNERETS OF THIS AFRICAN BLACK WIDOW SPIDER AS SHE SPINS HER WEB.

sheet, others are funnel-shaped, and some look like scaffolds.

The finest examples of web engineering are the beautiful structures made by orb-weaver spiders. These wheel-shaped webs consist of a dry-silk framework of "spokes" radiating out from a central "hub." On top

investigate. The spider's legs and feet are coated with a film of oil that stops it from getting stuck on its own silk. Arriving at the scene, the spider grabs the victim and wraps it up in

SPIDER SILK IS STRONGER THAN STEEL, STRETCHIER THAN RUBBER

of this framework the spiders lay a spiral of sticky silk.

When an insect blunders into the web, it's held tight by the gooey spiral. As it thrashes and wriggles in vain, vibrations pass along the threads to the spider, which scurries across the web to

silk. If the prey is an awkward customer—a stinging insect such as a wasp—the spider first gives it a paralyzing bite to subdue it. The spider may eat its prey on the spot, or leave the silk food parcel until it feels hungry.

TRAPDOOR SPIDERS DIG BURROWS USING THEIR FANGS, WHICH CARRY STRONG SPINES TO HELP LOOSEN THE SOIL.

SILK DOOR

Recycled webs

Some spiders only replace their webs when they get damaged, but orb-weavers spin a new web every night. However, spinning webs uses up a lot of energy and materials from the spider's body, so the old web is rolled up and eaten to recycle the nutrients it contains.

It's certainly worth making the effort to recycle—orb-weavers do an awful lot of spinning while they're alive. Garden spiders, which are orb-weavers, make 100 or more webs during their lifetime, each one taking about an hour to spin and using up to 300 ft (100 m) of silk!

Nets, lassos, and slings

Not all webs are so intricate. The net-casting spider makes a tiny, rectangular web, rather like a fishing net. Dangling on a thread above the ground, the spider uses the "net" to scoop up insects that pass underneath.

Some spiders don't bother with webs at all, but use their back legs to lasso their prey by flinging loops of sticky silk over them. And then there are bolas spiders, which hunt moths using a ball of sticky silk that they whirl around on a thread like a slingshot. The ball is coated with a chemical that mimics the mating scent of female moths.

When a male moth arrives, attracted by the fake scent, the spider takes aim, lets fly with its weapon, and hauls in its prize.

Burrows and pits

A trapdoor spider doesn't live in a web, but digs out a burrow in the soil, which it lines with silk. Then it builds a "door" from soil particles and silk, and fixes it to the burrow's entrance with a silk hinge. The spider hides in its burrow, behind the door, until it feels vibrations in the ground caused by the tiny feet of an approaching insect. In the blink of an eye, the spider dashes out, grabs its prey, and darts back down into its lair again.

The larva (young) of an insect called the ant-lion also excels at excavating. It digs a cone-shaped pit in sandy soil and buries itself at the bottom, with just its eyes and jaws showing. Sooner or later, a small insect puts a foot (or a few feet) wrong and falls into the hole. As the insect desperately tries to scramble back up the pit's steep sides, the larva starts flicking grains of sand at the insect with its mouthparts. The bombardment sends the insect tumbling down to the bottom of the pit…and into the larva's waiting jaws.

Worms with glue guns

Like the ant-lion, velvet worms also fire ammunition at prey— except that in this case the ammunition is not sand grains, but glue. These creepy-crawly gunslingers have a glue-squirting nozzle on

LOG ON…
www.explorit.org/
science/spider.html

HAVING TRAPPED A CRICKET WITH ITS GLUE SPRAY, A VELVET WORM MOVES IN TO START FEEDING.

either side of the mouth. They scour the floor of tropical forests at night to hunt for millipedes, spiders, insects, and other small creatures among the leaf debris. When a worm encounters prey, it sprays the victim with glue. The nozzles swing from side to side as they fire, coating the victim in a mass of sticky, criss-crossing threads. With its prey trapped, the velvet worm pierces the body with its claw-like jaws and injects digestive fluid.

Water cannons

Another sure shot is the archer fish, which lives in the mangrove swamps of Australia, Southeast Asia, and the Pacific Islands. This amazing fish has a built-in water cannon that can knock insects and spiders off waterside plants.

When it spots prey, the archer fish forms its mouth into a tube and then snaps its gill covers shut, shooting out a high-speed jet of water. This water cannon can accurately hit targets more than 3.5 ft (1 m) away. It obviously takes time to become such a sharpshooter, because young archer fish are often way off target. Their aim gradually improves with age and practice.

Sonic blasters

Some predators "shoot" at their prey with invisible ammunition! Sperm whales and dolphins fire

pulses of high-intensity sound, like low-pitched "bangs," at fish. Stunned and dazed by the force of the sonic blasts, the fish swim around in circles or just float motionless, and become easy pickings for the hunters. But without doubt the most incredible sound weapon of all belongs to a shrimp.

One of the pistol shrimp's

claws is extra-large—about half as long as its entire body. When the shrimp snaps the claw shut, tiny bubbles of water vapor form and then suddenly collapse with a noise that's loud enough to shatter glass! Pistol shrimp use the noise of the imploding bubbles to communicate with each other—and also to knock prey senseless. A quick click of the claw, and supper's ready.

Battery power

Sound travels well in water—as does electricity. Some fish, including the torpedo ray of the Pacific Ocean, can make their own electricity and use it as a devastating weapon. A torpedo ray has two large electric organs containing thousands of cells called electroplaques, which act as mini-batteries. Together they can produce a shock of up to 200 volts, which the ray can direct at its prey. The lethal dose of electricity causes the prey's muscles to

WEIRD WORLD

SOME GREEN HERONS HUNT WITH BAIT. THEY DROP AN INSECT INTO THE WATER AND SPEAR ANY FISH THAT COME TO CHECK IT OUT. IF THE BIRD HAS NO LUCK, IT PICKS UP ITS BAIT AND TRIES ELSEWHERE.

contract so fast that it breaks its own back.

The most potent electric fish is the Amazon electric eel of South America, which uses its shocking powers to kill frogs and fish. Its electric organs can discharge up to 650 volts—sufficient to prove deadly to any person or horse unlucky enough to be in the water at the time.

Animal hypnotists

If you can't trap, lasso, shoot down your prey, or stun it with a blast of sound or electricity, you can always hypnotize it! Stoats, weasels, and foxes seem to

ONE SNAP OF THE PISTOL SHRIMP'S HUGE CLAW PUTS NEARBY FISH OUT OF ACTION.

perform bizarre "dances" to
mesmerize prey. The dancer
makes strange sideways leaps,
chases its own tail, or runs
giddily around its victim, which
is entranced by the antics and
doesn't notice that the hunter is
gradually edging closer. All of a
sudden, the dancer stops the
performance and leaps on the
watching animal.

Cuttlefish don't dance, but
they too are superb hypnotists.
Like octopuses, they can change
color by flooding their skin
with pigment. When a cuttlefish
finds prey, bands of color wash
over the cuttlefish's body in a
bewitching spectacle that briefly
confuses the victim. When the
cuttlefish gets within range, its
suckered tentacles shoot out and
snatch the creature.

F atal attraction

Another piece of trickery is to
use a lure—something to tempt
an animal to come close enough
to be eaten. Australia's death
adder has a bright tip to its tail
that resembles a juicy worm,
caterpillar, or beetle grub.
When the snake wiggles this

EXPERTLY CAMOUFLAGED IN ITS DESERT
HABITAT, THE DEATH ADDER LIES WITH ITS
HEAD BESIDE THE BRIGHT LURE ON ITS TAIL.

colorful lure, birds, rodents, and lizards find it irresistible. If a hungry creature tries to eat the tasty morsel, the snake rewards it with a swift bite and a large injection of venom. The animal that arrived expecting to dine finds itself ending up as dinner!

Shell-crackers and tool-users

Sometimes a predator needs an extra trick up its sleeve to get at inaccessible food. For example, when a tortoise pulls its head and legs into its shell, it's well protected against an eagle's beak and claws. The eagle overcomes this problem by carrying the tortoise into the air and dropping it onto rocks. With luck (for the eagle!), the shell cracks and the bird gets to feast on the tasty meat inside.

A few predators even use everyday objects as simple tools to help them find food. Egyptian vultures, for example, break open ostrich eggs with stones, while sea otters use pebbles to smash their way into clam shells. Chimpanzees are also tool-users, "fishing" termites out of their nests with grass stems,

as are some small finches of the Galápagos Islands, which use cactus spines to hook grubs from tree bark.

There is almost an endless variety of hunting methods used by predators. Although many of them seem "cunning" or "clever," they are all just the result of animals following their instinct. But they're still pretty amazing!

AN EGYPTIAN VULTURE MAY FLY UP TO 3 MILES (5 KM) TO FIND A SUITABLE STONE FOR CRACKING OSTRICH EGGS.

SURVIVAL SKILLS

Running on water, squirting blood, and pretending to be dead are a few of the extreme tactics that animals use to escape tricky situations. The chances are that, sooner or later, every prey animal will find itself face to face with a hungry hunter. That's the moment when its life hangs in the balance. If the animal's survival skills are good enough, it will live to see another day. If they aren't...

Safety in numbers

Moving and feeding in large, tight-knit groups is an important survival tactic for some prey animals. In a group, there are many more pairs of eyes to watch out for danger. At the same time, predators find it very difficult to single out an

FOR DEFENSE IN THE OPEN OCEAN, FISH TRAVEL IN WELL-ORGANIZED SHOALS, SOMETIMES UP TO A MILLION STRONG.

individual for attack when the animals are clustered close together. What's more, if the group suddenly disperses, a predator may be confused by the sheer number of animals fleeing in all directions. That's one of the reasons why grazing mammals gather in herds on grassland, and why many marine fish swim in shoals.

Run for your life

Most animals, however, live solitary lives and have to fend for themselves. If an animal's life is at risk, its first instinct is to hot-foot it out of the danger zone. The basilisk lizard of Central America has a special trick to ensure that attackers won't give chase—it runs over water! When cornered by a predator, the basilisk jumps off its perch on a riverside branch and runs over the water's surface on its hind legs, supported by its broad-soled feet and the scaly fringes on its long toes. As the lizard loses speed it starts to sink, so it dives underwater and swims away to safety.

Look tough—or bluff!

If escape isn't possible, some animals adopt an aggressive pose to persuade predators to back off. In Australia, the Sydney funnel-web spider raises its front legs and exposes its venomous fangs, as if to say "If you want to fight, I'm ready!" Faced with such a threatening display, most predators beat a hasty retreat.

THE BASILISK LIZARD CAN TAKE UP TO 20 STRIDES PER SECOND AS IT SPRINTS OVER WATER TO AVOID PREDATORS.

Even if an animal isn't very
fearsome, it can always bluff.
Australia's frilled lizard, for
example, has a large flap of skin
around its neck, called a frill,
which normally lies flat, like
a closed umbrella. When
danger threatens, the lizard
raises the frill to make itself
appear much larger and more
fierce than it really is.

Playing dead

Acting tough works for certain
animals, but others stay alive by
pretending to be dead! This may
seem like an odd survival tactic,
but it works, because most
predators will only eat prey
that they've killed themselves.

The European grass snake is
especially good at feigning
death. It turns over on its back
and lets its body go limp. The
snake's eyes stare blankly, its
mouth gapes open, and its
tongue lolls out. To complete
the act, it releases a reeking
liquid from its anus, to mimic
the putrefying smells of a
rotting corpse. As
soon as the predator
heads off in
search of "live"
prey, the snake
drops the
pretense and
slithers away.

Buying time

Few animals
are such good
actors, so many rely
on shock tactics to win
themselves a few vital
seconds in which to make

THE FRILLED LIZARD'S DEFENSIVE DISPLAY
INVOLVES HISSING, RAISING ITS NECK
FRILL, AND LASHING ITS TAIL AROUND.

WHEN ESCAPE SEEMS IMPOSSIBLE, THE GRASS SNAKE FLIPS ITSELF ONTO ITS BACK AND PLAYS DEAD.

their getaway. Many frogs, for example, let out blood-curdling screams to startle their enemies. Three North American species of horned lizard go one better—they actually use their own blood (uncurdled) as a defensive weapon. By increasing their blood pressure, the lizards are able to burst blood vessels in their eye sockets and squirt a jet of the red stuff at assailants. It's enough to make most predators lose their appetite!

Body armor

You don't need fancy tricks if you're armor-plated. The three-banded armadillo of South America is covered in bony shields and toughened skin that protect it against the claws and teeth of its attackers. What's more, it can roll itself up into a tight ball, leaving no exposed legs, tail, or snout for a predator to grab.

Sharp spines are another way to make yourself difficult to eat. The spines, or "quills," of Africa's Cape porcupine are modified

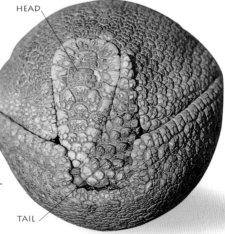

HEAD

TAIL

THE THREE-BANDED ARMADILLO CAN CURL UP INTO A BALL THAT MOST PREDATORS FIND IMPOSSIBLE TO BREAK INTO.

77

THIS LION HAS HAD A PAINFUL ENCOUNTER WITH A CAPE PORCUPINE, WHOSE BLACK-AND-WHITE QUILLS REMAIN STUCK IN THE LION'S FACE.

grasshoppers can spew out a mass of toxic foam from glands behind the head.

Spraying your chemicals rather than oozing them can ensure that your enemies don't get anywhere near you. The skunk can hit an attacker up to 16 ft (5 m) away with a foul-smelling spray fired from two nozzles on its backside. The spray is so repugnant that it's guaranteed to cause nausea and a rapid retreat. A direct hit in the eyes can even leave the attacker temporarily blinded.

F oul play

In fact, the more you find out about animal defenses, the more disgusting it gets.

A SKUNK'S SPRAY CAN BE SMELLED FROM 1 MILE (1.6 KM) AWAY

hairs that are only loosely attached to the skin. The porcupine drives the quills into an attacker's body so that they break off and lodge in its flesh.

C hemical defenses

Many animals use chemicals for their defense. Ladybugs, for example, can ooze a bitter-tasting fluid from their joints to ward off predators, while some

The fulmar, a cliff-nesting seabird, responds to threats by vomiting a stinking yellow oil over predatory birds such as sea eagles. And the oil doesn't just smell—it also seriously damages the feathers of the attacker.

But there's a fate worse than being vomited on for ravens and

WHEN A SKUNK RAISES ITS TAIL AND POINTS ITS BACKSIDE IN YOUR DIRECTION, YOU KNOW ITS TIME TO LEAVE THE SCENE!

magpies that try to raid the nests of small European birds called fieldfares. The fieldfares repeatedly dive-bomb the raiders with dollops of poop! It's messy, but effective.

THIS TREE SKINK LIZARD HAD TO SHED THE END OF ITS TAIL TO ESCAPE FROM AN ATTACKER.

Disposable body parts

Perhaps the most extreme tactic for getting out of sticky situations is to sacrifice parts of your body. When grabbed by the tail, many lizards are able to shed the tail and scamper off. To do this, the lizard simply contracts its tail muscles and the tail snaps at a specially weakened point.

The shocked predator is left with nothing but a piece of tail to snack on, while its main course, the lizard, lives to see another day. The lizard's tail grows back, but it's usually not as well-formed as the original version—a small price to pay for survival.

Shedding body parts to escape danger is not unique to lizards. Starfish can break off an arm that's been grasped by an attacker, and then grow it back again. But here's the staggering part—if the severed arm doesn't get eaten by the predator, it can develop into a complete new starfish. It's a bit like cloning yourself from a fingernail clipping!

PREDATORS AT RISK

We share planet Earth with an amazing array of animals—all of which are either predator or prey, or both. Sadly, we are making survival difficult for many animals and some are becoming increasingly scarce. As people clear land, they destroy habitats. Some species are threatened by hunters. Others are put at risk because people trade live animals, or animal parts, for money.

Habitat destruction

It's not just humans that need homes. Other animals, too, require somewhere to feed, shelter, and raise their young. The "home" of a wild animal is called its habitat. This is the natural environment in which the animal lives, and which provides it with all the things it needs to survive. The habitat of a lion, for example, is Africa's savannah grassland.

The trouble is, human activity is affecting habitats around the globe. As the human population grows, more and more of the Earth's surface is taken up with houses, factories, farms, and roads. To provide land for this rapid expansion, forests are cut down, grasslands are plowed up, and wetlands are drained.

CROCODILE AND ALLIGATOR SKINS ARE USED TO MAKE CLOTHES, SHOES, AND FASHION GOODS SUCH AS THIS PURSE.

Other habitats are flooded when dams are built across rivers, or torn apart when mines are excavated to extract minerals. As their habitats shrink, animal populations decrease, and some species are now facing extinction.

P oisoned food chains

Even when habitats are not being destroyed so that the land can be used for other purposes, they can still be seriously damaged by pollution. Every day, factories flush chemicals into rivers, cars belch out toxic exhaust fumes, oil and sewage are dumped into the sea, and waste is strewn over the land.

Pollution weakens animals by poisoning their food supplies. Toxic substances can build up in an animal's body until they reach dangerous levels. The toxins are passed on as animals eat each other, and become most concentrated in species at the top of the food chain, such as polar bears, birds of prey, and whales. Although the animals don't always die, the toxins may make them more susceptible to disease and affect their ability to breed.

VAST NUMBERS OF SHARKS, DOLPHINS, AND WHALES DIE ACCIDENTALLY WHEN THEY GET TANGLED IN FISHING NETS. THIS GREAT WHITE SHARK DIED IN A TUNA NET.

W ild harvest

Sometimes animals face a double threat—not only are their habitats at risk, but they are also targeted by hunters. Throughout history, people have hunted animals for food. Today, most meat comes from domesticated, farmed animals,

81

but hunting wild creatures for their flesh—"bushmeat"—is still important. In Africa, for example, hunters catch a wide range of animals for their meat, including crocodiles and chimpanzees. But if animals are

Hunting the hunters
Killing for food is common in the animal world, but humans have found many other reasons to hunt down the hunters.

THESE AFRICAN WILD DOGS ARE WEARING RADIO COLLARS, WHICH HELP SCIENTISTS TO LEARN MORE ABOUT THEIR LIFE IN THE WILD.

THERE ARE NOW ONLY 3,000–5,500 WILD DOGS LEFT IN AFRICA

killed faster than they can breed, their numbers dwindle, and the hunters' food source disappears.

Our greatest wild harvest is from the sea. Each year, millions of tons of marine creatures—including predators such as tuna, swordfish, sharks, and squid—are hauled from the ocean. But, like populations of land animals, fish stocks aren't inexhaustible. Overfishing of species such as cod and mackerel has made the fish so scarce that it's becoming difficult for trawlers to catch enough fish to fill their nets.

Often, the animals are killed because they're thought to be pests. For example, as farms and ranches replace the habitat of African wild dogs, the dogs increasingly can't find enough of their natural prey. As they search for other sources of food, they sometimes attack domestic animals such as cattle. Then the farmers shoot the dogs to protect their livestock.

Animals may also be hunted to supply materials for the fashion industry. Seals, foxes, jaguars, and leopards are taken for their fur, while snakes, lizards, and crocodiles are hunted for their skin. The Siamese crocodile has now disappeared from parts of Southeast Asia as a result of the trade in its hide.

Other animals are hunted because their body parts are valued in traditional medicine. The gallbladders of Asiatic black bears and the bones of tigers, for example, are used as ingredients in tonics and potions to treat a variety of illnesses.

The pet trade
Some people enjoy keeping unusual pets, such as bird-eating spiders, chameleons, pythons, and even bears and chimpanzees. To meet the demand, live animals are taken from the wild and smuggled to other countries

to be sold. This trade has brought about the decline of some species in the wild.

Hope for the future
The future may look bleak, but all is not lost, because much is being done to help endangered species. To safeguard habitats,

ARMED GUARDS KEEP A WATCH FOR POACHERS IN AN INDIAN NATIONAL PARK.

WEIRD WORLD

BY THE EARLY 1970S, THERE WERE ONLY 5,000 WILD TIGERS IN ASIA. CONSERVATION PROGRAMS HELPED THE TIGER POPULATION TO REACH 7,000, BUT NUMBERS ARE NOW FALLING AGAIN DUE TO POACHING.

thousands of national parks and wildlife reserves have been set up throughout the world. These are places where animals can live and breed in safety, and where the land (or sea) is set aside for nature conservation.

What's more, governments have made agreements to limit pollution, control or even ban the trade in live animals and animal body parts, and regulate fishing industries.

The demand for some animal products—such as the skins of crocodiles, or the fur of foxes— is met by raising the animals in farms. This doesn't stop animals from being killed, but it does help to protect wild populations.

Even when a species is on the verge of dying out, zoologists may still be able to save it by breeding the animals in zoos and then releasing them into the wild. In the US, these "captive breeding" programs have already helped to save the California condor and the red wolf from extinction.

Play your part

There's plenty more still to do if many of the world's animals— predators and prey alike—aren't to be relegated to the history books. We can all play our part by getting involved with wildlife groups that work to protect animals at risk.

TOURISTS IN THE MASAI MARA NATIONAL PARK, KENYA, ENJOY THE THRILL OF SEEING A MALE LION IN ITS NATURAL HABITAT.

REFERENCE SECTION

Whether you've finished reading *Predator*, or are turning to this section first, you'll find the information on the next eight pages really helpful. Here are all the facts and figures, background details, and unfamiliar words that will notch up your knowledge. You'll also find a list of website addresses—so whether you want to surf the net or search out facts, these pages should turn you from an enthusiast into an expert.

CLASSIFYING PREDATORS

In order to discuss all the different species of animal and plant, scientists classify them into a series of categories according to the features that they share. In classification, the largest categories are called kingdoms. There are a total of five kingdoms. Predators belong to the kingdom Animalia, which includes every animal species. Kingdoms are divided into smaller categories, which are further divided until individual species are reached. This chart shows the classification of the gray wolf.

Kingdom: Animalia
Multicelled organisms that obtain energy by eating food. Most are mobile.

Phylum: Chordata
Animals with a strengthening backbone or rod in their bodies. Contains 5 classes.

Class: Mammalia
At least 21 orders of hairy, warm-blooded animals with backbones, that suckle their young.

Order: Carnivora
This contains 7 families of mammals with specialized teeth for biting and shearing. Most are predators.

Family: Canidae
There are 36 species of doglike animals. Most have muscular bodies, long legs, and bushy tails.

Genus: *Canis*
The 8 *Canis* species include wolves, coyotes, jackals, and the domestic dog.

Species: *Canis lupus*
The gray wolf is an intelligent predator that lives in family groups called packs.

FOOD CHAINS

Most food chains begin with plants, which get their energy from sunlight. This diagram shows a food chain for an orca. It begins with phytoplankton, which are microscopic plants that float in the ocean. These plants are consumed by tiny ocean creatures called zooplantkton, which in turn are eaten by squid, and so on.

Orcas feed on several hundred species, from seals, turtles, and fish to whales and sea otters, so they form part of many different food chains. Phytoplankton are at the bottom of almost every ocean food chain, so they are vital to marine life.

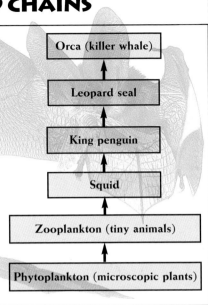

Orca (killer whale)

↑

Leopard seal

↑

King penguin

↑

Squid

↑

Zooplankton (tiny animals)

↑

Phytoplankton (microscopic plants)

WEBSITES

www.howstuffworks.com/animal-camouflage.htm
Cool site on the ins and outs of animal camouflage.

www.uen.org/utahlink/activities/view_activity.cgi?activity_id=3803
Questions on animal defenses, and links to websites that hold the solutions.

www.arcytech.org/java/population/facts_foodchain.html
Plenty of interesting facts, plus diagrams, about food chains and food webs.

www.boomerwolf.com/wolfwrld.htm
Hear wolves sing, find out how they hunt, discover what games they play.

www.pauldfrost.btinternet.co.uk/index.html
Fascinating site about birds of prey, with links.

www.5tigers.org
All about tigers, the threats they face, and what can be done to help them.

www.enchantedlearning.com/subjects/whales
All you ever wanted to know about orcas and other whale species.

www.bbc.co.uk/reallywild/amazing
An A–Z of nature's most amazing animals. Click on a letter and take your pick.

www.worldalmanacforkids.com/explore/animals/ant.html
In-depth information about ants, including army ants.

RECORDS AND FEATS

Largest ocean predator
Blue whale. Adult males average
82 ft (25 m) and up to 130 tons.

Largest land predator
Polar bear. Adult males typically
weigh 880–1,300 lb (400–600 kg),
with a nose-to-tail length of
95–102 in (2.4–2.6 m). Grizzly bears
occasionally reach similar sizes.

Smallest predator
There are microscopic, single-celled
"hunters" called protozoans that
devour other protozoans for food.
However, these minute life forms
don't behave quite like animal
predators because they don't have
eyes, ears, or even mouths! Among
the smallest true animal predators
are pseudoscorpions, which can
measure just 0.06 in (1.5 mm) long.
They grab springtails and other tiny
animals with their venomous pincers.

Fastest flier
Peregrine falcon, which can attain
speeds of more than 125 mph
(200 km/h) in a dive, or "stoop."
There are claims that it can even
reach up to 170 mph (270 km/h).

Fastest land predator
The cheetah. Over short distances—
up to 1,600 ft (500 m)—it can
achieve 60–63 mph (96–100 kmh).

Fastest ocean predator
The sailfish. This fish has a top speed
in excess of 62 mph (100 km/h).
Marlin and tuna are almost as fast.

Most efficient mammal scavenger
Most mammal predators consume
40 percent of their kill, but a spotted
hyena eats nearly 100 percent. Its
digestive system breaks down bones,
hooves, horns, and hides.

Longest-living predator
Fin whales can probably survive for
100 years, but some experts think
that crocodilies and alligators may
be able to live for up to 200 years.

Longest land predator
The reticulated python of southeast
Asia often exceeds 20.5 ft (6.25 m).
The greatest ever recorded length
was 32.5 ft (10 m) in Indonesia.

Most toxic snake
Hydrophis belcheri, a sea snake of the
Austro-Pacific region, has venom 100
times more toxic than that of any
land snake—0.000000.2 oz (0.005 mg)
would kill a 150-lb (70-kg) man.

Largest spiderwebs
These are made by tropical golden
orb-weavers of the genus *Nephila*,
and can be up to 10 ft (3 m) long.

Longest fast
In one rather cruel experiment, an
Asiatic pit viper survived 3 years and
3 months without eating.

Strongest spider
Californian trapdoor spiders can
resist a force up to 38 times their
own weight attempting to open the
door to their burrows.

ENDANGERED PREDATORS

Here are just a few of the many animals described as being "critically endangered" in the Red List produced by the International Union for the Conservation of Nature and Natural Resources (IUCN).

Vaquita (*Phocoena sinus*)
This porpoise is found only in the Gulf of California, off Mexico. It is on the brink of extinction, with only 100–500 vaquitas left in the wild. Main threats are hunting, habitat loss, pollution, and entanglement in fishing nets.

Iberian lynx (*Lynx pardinus*)
Fewer than 600 individuals surviving in Spain and Portugal. Main threats are habitat loss and dramatic decline of its rabbit prey.

Chinese alligator (*Alligator sinensis*)
This small crocodilian is found on China's Chang Jiang River. About 1,000 exist in the wild. Main threats are habitat destruction and hunting.

Philippine eagle (*Pithecophaga jefferyi*)
The wild population of this ferocious-looking, monkey-eating eagle is between 350 and 650. Main threat is the loss of its forest habitat.

Black-browed albatross (*Thalassarche melanophrys*)
This bird breeds on islands off the tip of South America and around Antarctica. Its numbers have declined by 40 percent in the last 30 years. Main threat is from long-line fishing nets, which ensnare the birds.

Golden Monteverde toad (*Bufo periglenes*)
This toad lives in a single forest in Costa Rica, but hasn't been seen since 1989. Main threat is the climate change caused by polluting gases (global warming).

Golden lancehead (*Bothrops insularis*)
This snake occurs only on Queimada Grande island off the coast of Brazil. Main threat is habitat destruction as a result of fires to clear the land.

Common sawfish (*Pristis pristis*)
This fish has a long snout edged with sawlike teeth. Mostly limited to the Atlantic off western Africa. Main threat is accidental capture in fishing nets.

Malaysian water shrew (*Chimarrogale hantu*)
This small mammal predator lives only in one forest on the Malay peninsula. Main threat is human encroachment into its habitat.

CONSERVATION ORGANIZATIONS

If you want to do something to save endangered animals—both predators and prey—there are lots of organizations you can join that will help you to get involved. You can either write to them or visit them on the internet.

Australian Conservation Federation
A campaigning group that works to protect Australian habitats.
340 Grove Street, Fitzroy, Melbourne, Vic 3065, Australia
www.acfonline.org.au/asp/pages/home.asp

Canadian Wildlife Federation
This organization sponsors research, funds wildlife projects, and raises awareness of wildlife issues.
350 Michael Coupland Drive, Kanata, Ontaria K2M 2W1, Canada
www.cwf-fcf.org

National Wildlife Federation
A US organization that aims to unite individuals, groups, and government to protect habitats and wildlife.
11100 Wildlife Center Drive, Preston, VA 20190-5362
www.nwf.org

International Union for the Conservation of Nature and Natural Resources (IUCN)
You can search the IUCN's Red List database of endangered species.
Rue Mauberney 28, CH-1196 Gland, Switzerland
www.iucn.org OR www.redlist.org

TRAFFIC International
TRAFFIC works to enforce laws that restrict the trade in live animals for the pet trade and animal parts for fashion and medicine.
1250 24th Street N.W., Washington, D.C. 20037-1175
www.traffic.org

Whale and Dolphin Conservation Society
A charity campaigning to protect whales, dolphins and porpoises.
Alexander House, James Street West, Bath NA1 2BT, UK
www.wdcs.org

Wildlife Protection Society of India
Campaigns against the illegal trade in tigers and other wildlife
M-52 Greater Kailash Part - I, New Delhi 110048, India
www.wpsi-india.org

Wildlife Trusts Partnerships
Charity caring for more than 2,400 nature reserves in the UK and campaigns for wildlife protection.
The Kiln, Waterside, Mather Road, Newark, Notts NG 24 1WT, UK
www.wildlifetrusts.org/mainframe.php

Worldwide Fund for Nature
Visit the website to find out what WWF is doing for predators at risk.
1250 24th Street N.W., Washington, D.C. 20037-1175
www.panda.org

GLOSSARY

Algae (singular—alga)
Simple organisms that live like plants, by collecting energy from sunlight.

Antennae (singular—antenna)
The "feelers" of crustaceans and insects that detect touch and smell.

Bacteria (singular—bacterium)
Microscopic, one-celled organisms.

Camouflage
The way that animals use shape and color to blend in with their surroundings and hide from view.

Captive breeding
Breeding animals in captivity, and then releasing them into the wild.

Carcass
The dead body of an animal.

Carnivores
Meat-eating animals.

Carrion
The flesh of a dead animal.

Cells
Tiny structures that are the building blocks of all organisms. Most animals and plants contain millions of cells.

Chromatophores
Skin cells that contain pigments.

Cnidarian
An animal without a backbone that has stinging tentacles, such as jellyfish and anemones. Cnidarians use a single body opening to feed and excrete.

Cold-blooded animal
An animal, such as a fish, frog, lizard, or insect, whose body temperature changes with that of its surroundings.

Compound eye
An eye found in crustaceans and insects that is made up of many separate units, called ommatidia, each of which contains a lens.

Conservation
Work to protect animals, plants, and their habitats.

Constrictor
A snake that wraps its body around its victims and suffocates them.

Counter-shading
Camouflage used by many fish and marine creatures. It consists of a dark upper body and lighter undersides.

Crustacean
An animal without a backbone, such as a crab or shrimp, that has jointed legs and two pairs of antennae.

Detrivores
Organisms that feed on dead remains.

Distant touch
The ability of animals such as spiders, scorpions, and fish to sense the vibrations made by creatures moving some distance away.

Echolocation
Making sounds and using the echoes to find prey or navigate.

Electroplaques
Electricity-producing cells found in skates and rays. Electroplaques are used to stun prey with electric shocks.

Electroreceptors
Sensory cells in animals such as sharks and rays that can detect the weak electrical signals produced by the muscles of other creatures.

Enzymes
Proteins that speed up chemical reactions in living things.

Fangs
Specialized teeth for injecting or chewing venom into prey.

Food chain
A series of links in which energy and

nutrients pass from one living thing to the next as organisms feed.

Food web
A collection of food chains.

Fungi (singular—fungus)
Living things that absorb food from dead matter around them.

Gills
Organs for breathing underwater.

Habitat
The surroundings and resources that a living thing needs to survive.

Heat pits
Organs on the heads of some snakes that can detect the body heat of prey.

Herbivores
Animals that eat plants.

Gland
An organ that produces chemicals to control body processes.

Instinct
A type of built-in behavior that an animal inherits from its parents.

Invertebrate
An animal without a backbone.

Jacobson's organ
A scent-detecting organ in the mouths of snakes and some lizards.

Krill
Tiny, shrimplike creatures.

Larva (plural—larvae)
A young animal that looks very different from its parents, and that lives in a different way. A larva changes as it grows up.

Lateral line
A line along a fish's body containing sensory cells. It detects vibrations made by animals in the water.

Lens
A transparent structure that focuses light rays to form an image.

Lure
A body part, such as the wiggling tip

of a tail, that a predator uses to tempt prey to come closer.

Mammal
A hairy, warm-blooded animal with a backbone. All female mammals suckle their young. Humans, bears, cats, dogs, and cattle are mammals.

Mollusk
A soft-bodied animal without a backbone, often protected by a hard shell. Snails, slugs, squid, and most shellfish are mollusks.

Nectar
A sweet liquid produced by flowers. Many insects feed on nectar.

Nervous system
A system of interconnected nerve cells that collects information from an animal's body, and sends out instructions to control it.

Nutrients
Substances that a living thing needs in order to grow and stay healthy. Nutrients are obtained from food.

Omnivores
Animals that eat both plants and meat.

Organ
A self-contained body part with a special function, such as the brain or the heart.

Organism
Anything that is alive.

Parasitic
Living and feeding on or inside another organism.

Photoreceptors
Sensory cells in an animal's eyes that can detect light.

Pollen
Dustlike plant particles that contain the male sex cells of a flower.

Pollution
The contamination of air, land, and water by toxic gases and chemicals.

Predators
An animal that kills other creatures for food.

Prey
Anything caught by a predator.

Primate
A mammal with flexible fingers and toes, and forward-pointing eyes. Monkeys and apes (including humans) are primates.

Proteins
Substances produced by living cells. Proteins are essential for life. Some proteins control chemical processes, others are used as building materials.

Reptile
A cold-blooded animal with a backbone and a dry, scaly skin. Snakes, lizards, turtles, and crocodiles are all reptiles.

Retina
A lining at the back of the eyes of mammals and birds that is packed with light-detecting cells.

Saliva
A liquid, produced in or near the mouth, that helps break down food.

Scavengers
Animals that feed on the bodies of dead animals.

Silk
A type of protein produced by spiders that is used for building webs, capturing prey, and much more.

Simple eye
A type of primitive eye that can only detect differences in light and shade.

Species
A group of organisms with similar features that can breed with each other but not with anything else.

Smell receptors
Sensory cells in an animal's nose that can detect scents in air or water.

Social animals
Animals that live together in groups.

Spinal cord
A column of nervous tissue that relays information between the body and brain of a vertebrate animal.

Stalking
A hunting tactic in which a predator slowly creeps up on its prey until it is within striking distance.

Stereoscopic vision
The way that an animal's brain uses the overlapping views from its two eyes to form 3-D images.

Stinger
The sharp body part of animals such as scorpions, wasps, and ants that injects poison into prey or attackers.

Tapetum
A reflective layer at the back of some animals' eyes, which enables them to see better at night.

Thermoreceptors
Sensory cells in the heat pit of a snake or lizard that can detect tiny changes in the external temperature.

Toxins
Poison produced by living things.

Venom
A poison produced by an animal, and injected or stabbed into another creature by a sting or a bite.

Vertebrate
An animal with a backbone.

Warm-blooded animal
An animal that can keep its body at the same temperature all the time. It does this by breaking down food or stored body fat to produce heat.

Warning colors
Bright, contrasting colors used by an animal to warn its enemies that it is poisonous or able to give a painful bite or sting.

INDEX

CREDITS

Dorling Kindersley would like to thank:
Dean Price for the jacket design and Chris Bernstein for compiling the index.

Additional photography by:
Geoff Brightling, Jane Burton, Geoff Dann, Frank Greenaway, Dave King, Karl Shone, Kim Taylor, Jerry Young.